NATURALIST ON WATCH

Alton A. Lindsey

W9-DCB-650

You have jumped off, you know not how, into the dark wide mystery of time, where the past is vastly alive, and the future is not separated off.

—D.H. Lawrence
The Man Who Loved Islands

Published by
MERRY LEA ENVIRONMENTAL
LEARNING CENTER
GOSHEN COLLEGE
Goshen, IN 46526

Note for Libraries:
This book is printed on a 60 lb., *acid-free*, long-lasting paper, and need not be treated for removal of acid residues.

Library of Congress Catalog Card Number: 83-62027

International Standard Book Number (ISBN): 0-913859-00-1 for Hardcover version; 0-913859-01-x for Paperback.

Printed in the United States of America

NATURALIST ON WATCH

DEDICATED TO

LEE A. RIETH

MARY JANE RIETH

Builders, Nature-lovers and preservers,
who founded and sustain Merry Lea Center

CONTENTS

PROLOGUE
FINDING LIFE BETWEEN COMETS

WHAT a naturalist knows tends to be what he sees. Unquestionably, many things crucial and trivial, deliberate and random, happened before the night in 1910 when I saw Halley's Comet, but I cannot vouch for any of them. My earliest memory of any kind is an evening scene composed around a central heavenly splendor.

This three-year-old knew security, held up on the shoulders of a strong young father whose right hand held the mother's hand. They stood knee-deep in meadow grass beneath a cloud-free night. Slantwise above the black silhouette of a neighbor's barn hung the legendary comet, trailing across the sky from brilliance at our right to gauzy unreality eastward.

The boy did not know that he was seeing the sovereign flag of our sun's vast system, whipped out incandescent in the lee of the solar wind. Nor did he foresee that this appearance and the one to follow after seventy-six years would essentially form the frame around his past-conscious existence.

No one then knew of the debt that we all may owe to comet kind. It was perhaps a certain ancient comet which, though seen by no human eyes then or later, made this planet safe for humanity. Some scientists now think that the catastrophe which ended the horrendous Age of Dinosaurs was an impact that darkened the atmosphere for several years. They believe that the head of a comet struck the Earth near Iceland; others think it may have been a large asteroid. A track it seems to have left behind is a widespread stratum of clay in various parts of the world, too rich in iridium to have been of terrestrial origin. Whether comet or asteroid, they speculate that its impact changed conditions too drastically for any dinosaurs to survive. Small, skulking mammals had long coexisted with those reptiles, but it seems quite inconceivable that anything like the human species could have arisen in a world with practically all ecological niches dominated by a great variety of dinosaurs.

It is nearly time now for Halley's Comet to return. To human beings, caught in the busy, crowded niche we made for ourselves within the siderial clockwork, Time is a relative thing. When one is young, the days are short and the years are long. When one is old, the days are long and the years are short. Some people say they are not interested in what went on in the past. This seems strange, for the present is ephemeral and the future is an unstable, floating dock for tying up our existential vessel.

I find the idea of Time a tricky one, more so than that of Space even though the two are closely related. While some philosophers think that Time is an illusion, for practical purposes our common sense and demonstrations of change support the reality of Time. As Georgescu-Roegan wrote, "The peculiarly unique feature of Time is its fleeting nature combined with its ever-presentness. Time flows, yet it is always present." It flows through our consciousness, and through the unconscious biological clocks of other living things. Scientists, but not all philosophers, think that Time pre-dated Man and thus exists independently of human consciousness. Time moves in only one direction—forward. It is irreversible, for all practical purposes. We cannot say how we stand at present on the scale of Time, because we don't know when zero-Time was. Was there a Time before the universe began?

My lifelong avocational interest is in conservation and Nature preservation. These involve hoping, planning, and working, in the light of the past, to organize the present in the interest of a good future. Idealistic humanists call for a "better" future for mankind, but I have heard of no one who thinks that Nature will become better in the future than it has been in the past. Naturalists who have lived long enough to have seen wild America nearer to mint condition do not expect that to be surpassed in times to come. What clearly can be improved is our stewardship and management of land and the diverse life it supports.

The solar wind chill and other factors of cosmic climatology appear favorable for the spring of 1986, when the comet is expected back amid a spectacular shower of meteors. Our forecast is for generally clear skies, diamond-faceted stars to the northward, and on Earth much sharp focusing on Halley's Comet with and without optical aids.

During that sky-watch we expect to have plenty of Time to review our sightings and findings since this comet's previous visit. There are many such things that may come to mind . . .

1

RAINBOWS, MIRAGES, AND MYSTERIES

DESPITE much wandering in desert country, traditional scene of mirage effects, I have seen only one mirage there. At the head of the Gulf of California, some trick of refraction seemed to lift the bare, brown mudflats of the Colorado River Delta, and to cystallize their images into vertical, narrow units of mirage. The illusion was given of a vast, crowded marshland of nothing but gigantic brown, cattail-like plants. My companion Natt Dodge, who headed the naturalist work in all the Southwestern National Monuments, had never seen or heard of such a mirage, either. All other specimens in my mirage collection come from the polar regions, north and south. Mountains or islands, actually far beyond the horizon, may be loomed into visibility by light refraction. How could early explorers near the ends of the earth have been expected to make accurate maps?

For threading an ice-breaking ship through the antarctic pack ice, overcast skies are most helpful. The open, ice-free leads are reflected as dark bands of "water sky" upon the bottom of the cloud stratum far ahead of the bowsprit. Conversely, in a largely open sea one may locate large masses of ice long before they become directly visible. The lighter tone of the cloud layer above them is termed "ice blink." Thus, the old term "sky pilot" carries a different connotation in polar waters.

Only the captain and I were on watch abovedecks when the *Pacific Fir* was steaming toward the Ross Ice Barrier in the early morning of January 17, 1934. I strained my gaze ahead for the first sight of the sheer white cliff rearing 250 feet out of the southernmost Ross Sea. Before that day, our expedition had not been anywhere near the great shelf ice formation, as large as France. At 6:16, I detected the first glimmer of the continuous ice-band on the horizon. Two minutes later the sharp, clear precipice was seen floating in the sky, apparently disconnected from the sea below it. This mirage, in which a strip of deep blue sky separates the white ice from the gray-green sea, has long been known as "Barrier looming."

Nearly all the rocky underpinning of Antarctica lies hidden beneath glacial ice and the newer snows. The works of man are still insignificant in that vast landscape. If most people who go there hate the place, as Dr. Paul Siple said, they must have looked above the horizon seldom. One atmospheric effect of rare beauty is much more frequent there than in temperate climes—mother of pearl clouds. The cloud cover of much of the sky near the obscured sun may assume variegated pastel coloring like that in clam shells.

As the eye sees things, no bright days anywhere on earth are brighter. Without dark glasses, or at least narrow-slitted eye-shields patterned after those made of shell by Eskimos at the opposite end of the world, one would very soon be snow-blinded. The brightness of sunny days may be excited further by the coruscating sparkle of the unusual "diamond dust" phenomenon. I have seen this remarkable sight only in Antarctica, and near the coast. The necessary moisture in the air comes from the open sea. When an air mass of high humidity is caught by a sudden drop to a much lower temperature, it forms not snow but a universe of visible ice needles, twisting slowly downward through the bright calm air.

The most spectacular sky effects of the austral summer are the organized and mathematically-determined halos. It is tempting to call them what they seem to be—colorful rainbows—but they are seen in skies that never experience rain. The halos depend on the refractive index of hexagonal ice crystals in the upper atmosphere, though they sometimes coincide with abundant diamond-dust about one's head.

The polar halo effects are elaborations of the sun-dog (parhelion) effect which may be seen in winter, infrequently but not really rarely, in our usual northern hemisphere haunts. Two weak and diffuse false suns appear at the same height as the real sun between them, and 22° out from it along the 360° circle of the horizon. There must be at least thin ice-clouds in those positions; one may see only one sun-dog if the sky is clear at the other degree position. A simple sun-dog, sometimes accompanied by a soft pillar of rosy light reaching up from the real sun a short way, is the farthest developed halo effect that I have seen outside of Antarctica.

At Little America, we often saw much more in summer. During my first day driving a dog team, when Admiral Byrd first hitched a ride on my sledge (surely among his most intrepid exploits), I saw my first ice-crystal halos. The sun-dogs were merely swollen parts of a single broad rainbow-circle with a 22° radius and reaching skyward at a right angle to the circle of horizon. Our ambient air was filled with falling ice crystals as well, an unforgettable vision.

On a later day I saw much more spectacular halo displays—a skyful of "rainbows." A complete bright ring of spectral colors (the parhelic circle) paralleled the horizon at the sun's elevation. Along this ring and 22° out from the sun in each horizontal direction was a brilliant sun-dog, a part of a complete vertical sky-wheel. Directly above the sun was an upper tangent arc lifting its two horns upward from the 22° ring, and, dropping away from the ring below the sun was a lower tangent arc. At the same time there were third and fourth sun-dogs forming parts of a second, more gigantic sky-wheel out 46° along the horizontal or parhelic circle. The outer wheel circled outside of and parallel to the 22° halo ring. Physics and aesthetics were co-producing a rare show on the illimitable antarctic stage.

There are a number of additional types of polar halos which I have not yet witnessed. Infralateral arcs may form as tangent arcs to the lower left and right sides of the 46° circle. There are reflection halos as well as the commoner refraction halos. The variety of one-, two-, and three-dimensional halos is astonishing, as is the complexity of the mathematical theory underlying them. Many refraction halos owe their existence to a kind of "bunching" of the light leaving the ice crystals, concentrating the light in certain directions, according to a theory termed "singularities of a mapping." Crystals may be randomly oriented as they drift downward, resulting in circular, three-dimensional halos, or they may fall in special orientations to produce various non-circular halos.

In mid-March, after penguins and all flying birds had gone north for the winter, the last sun-dogs seen were of brilliant gold light, climaxing a protracted sunset of rose, blue, and gold that filled the whole sky and flooded the Barrier snows with color. One of these splashes of false sun was hidden from time to time behind silhouetted pressure pinnacles of such fantastic forms that the place became known as Gnome-man's Land. There, while I skinned specimen seals at temperatures about minus 35 ° F., a mirror would show white frozen patches on my face which would then be kneaded pink again by bared fingers. On trips out from the base with more than one man, we would watch and warn each other. In the winter night, the lowest temperature I read from the alcohol thermometer outdoors was minus 78 ° F., at Little America's latitude of 78 ° South.

After the seasonal curtain of the atmospheric stage closed on daylight sky effects, it opened on the even more fabulous show presented in darkness by the sun's electron stream and the earth's magnetic field. In the dark months of the austral winter, the *aurora australis* exhibits Antarctica's ultimate beauty. Unlike the fixed halos, the beauty is that of constant movement as well as changing colors. Many observers have tried to convey its fragility, sweep, color, and changes, but no description, painting, or photograph I have seen appears worth the effort. Not the least salutary effect of watching the southern lights over the Barrier snows is the conviction that man-made art is basically derivative, second-hand stuff.

The extensive network of directional radio antennae at the base camp made it possible to hear the aurora as well as see it. Three of us watched the sky outdoors while fitted with earphones hooked up properly to the antenna system. Over the crackling associated with occasional bright meteors as they fell toward earth, we heard the swishing hiss intensify each time the aurora brightened. In combination, these amplified sounds seemed to represent "The creaking of the tented sky/The ticking of eternity," of which the poet Millay wrote.

As etherial and mysterious as auroral displays can seem, we encountered in Alaska in 1975 a phenomenon that was really inexplicable. For what particles or waves can propagate through the atmosphere or the earth's mantle a message pulsing from Indiana to Alaska for uninstrumented reception?

We were camped, Elizabeth and I, at the Portage Glacier near Anchorage, that night before we heard that an Alaskan Brown Bear had recently killed and eaten a college student there, trapped in his sleeping bag. My wife had a dream, of a sort unprecedented for her. Her mother, ninety years old and living in a retirement home, was reaching out to her and calling "Help me!" The next letter from dear old Louisa told of falling in the corridor outside her room, a unique experience for her in that safe haven. This had happened on the same date as the unpleasant dream. Could there possibly be, circling far out there somewhere, a signal-reflecting satellite of a kind we know nothing about?

From a canoe on Great Bear Lake north of the Arctic Circle, the Indian guide Blondin and I saw a strange mirage along the distant, rocky, treeless shoreline. The substantive materials were the bays and promontories, and the varied rocky cliffs in sunlight and shadow, together with their mirror images in the motionless lake, seen in sharp focus except where a linear mirage spread and blurred them where water and land met. When one inclined his head, shifting the view through ninety degrees to make it appear vertical, the two-part, symmetrical image now appeared to form an erect totem pole figure. The mirage effect between these halves was confusing reality into an amorphous brownish band connecting the land and its reflection, the whole creating a long series of faces—human, animal and often simian—one above another until the observer brought his head back to normal posture. I thought that such a sight might have furnished ancient Indians of the North their original inspiration for the totem pole, but I could not ask Blondin his views since we had no language in common.

During many tedious hours of our return trip, the windless, cloudless sky was colored identically with the lake. Except where the canoe disturbed the water, or a rare floating bubble marked the immaculate surface, it was impossible to tell, on the landless horizon or closer, at what level the water left off and the sky began. Huddled in the bow against the dead-calm chill, resigned to temporary torpor hour after uneventful hour, I had no stimulus except the hypnotic low hum of the outboard motor. That seemed like the background music of the spheres as I presumably entered into what would now be regarded as mild hypothermia—a state like that of entranced mystics who free their spirits from the discomfited flesh and reach a receptivity above rationality. In an undifferentiated uniformity of environment, with the cold blue of sea merging imperceptibly into the blue cold of sky, I felt as though plunging through endless reaches of impalpable Space. This must be what saints were wont to experience during their transcendence—the mindless, blissful merging of individual with universe to be known only in the depths and heights of mystical ecstacy. Or was it more like the other-worldly vision of beauty reported by those who have been snatched back at the last possible moment from incipient death?

The spell, certainly the closest I have come to the "religious experience" we hear about, was broken at last. We were again in a mundane canoe and nearing the uranium capital in Canada's Northwest Territories.

When our son David was eleven, we went on an ecological research trip to the virgin forests of northern Ontario, just south of the James Bay extension of Hudson's Bay. Our first day of work was so tiring that Dave went to bed soon after supper. After night had fallen completely, the northern sky staged a veil-dance of summer aurora for entrancing hours, as splendid as any aurora I had seen in the far south. Dave simply had to see this. I shook him, pummeled him, and yelled at him to awaken. It was quite impossible to wake the boy up without hurting him too much!

When I told him about it during breakfast, he was bitterly disappointed to have missed the show. He then stated flatly,

"If it comes out again tonight, you won't have any trouble getting me to wake up. I will wake up and see it!" That night a magnificent display of northern lights began a couple of hours after he fell asleep. Wondering about what he had said so categorically, I just touched him gently and said, "Aurora, Dave." He immediately jumped out of bed, as spry as a jack-in-the-box. We had come north to look for high points of Nature; there are strange depths to be found in Man.

2

DRUMMER, THE IROQUOIS
HEART-BEAT BIRD

THE Cay-oo-gah village, with its wigwams and maize
fields, slumbered in the strip of land between the stream and
a windfall of firewood downed by a tornado. Beyond it
glinted the long water which points its finger toward the
North Star. Silently the youth left the village, when the night

was darkest before the most important day of his life, to find his chosen totem, a lifelong profession, and a new name.

Some months before, he had been invited to the place of the old sachem, who was searching for an eventual successor. Standing before the wizened medicine man, he heard this:

Our warriors wear feathers of the noble Eagle upon their heads, whence come their strategy and guile during the raids. The hunters of our clan dangle from their wrists the fan-feathers of the wily Turkey, for the hands of men give them skills to provide the food-bird, the deer, the bear. However, we medicine men command the most respect of all men. We and our totem-bird stand for the heart, where the most vital wisdom and deepest mysteries lie buried.

It is a splendid bird, our totem of the quiet lore about small growing things of the Earth, the simples, which we sachems put to use to save lives. Young one, place your ear against my chest and say to me what you hear!

It was like the sound that he had often heard to throb through the greening woods in the Mating Moon—the beat of the proud, wise, wary Drummer. When the fragrant Arbutus peeps from beneath its harsh leaves, then the bird from its heart calls to the heart of its mate, "Come to the drum log, come." The bird acts strangely during the Mad Moon also, after the wavy yellow ribbons of the witch-hazel have unfurled, but before the deep snows muffle the ground. Then the dignity and poise of the Heart-beat bird desert him in his despairing frenzy over the passing of the fruitful autumn.

The youth's fateful mission this night was to watch and learn how the Drummer makes his unbirdlike notes. If able to find the answer known to established sachems, he could begin serious preparations as apprentice to the old one, to be taught the healing simples, how to make decoctions from forest herbs, and how also the heart can cure the ailing body by longing for life.

13

The young Iroquois made his careful way far off, where no dog sounds of the village or snoring of the elders were near. Earlier he had scouted a spot where Drummer-sign showed that a large log was being used again this springtime. His approach was such that Drummer, if roosting in the hemlocks near the log, would be unlikely to detect human presence. He fitted his lithe body into a hollow of similar width, lying on last year's leaves and drawing others over him. Soon his breathing had become shallow and silent. When morning light arose, his skin, dark bronze like that of all two-legged unbirds in his world, would blend with the dead leaves. His black hair was obscured by evergreen fern fronds tied to his head. The West Wind, East Wind, South Wind and North Wind had smoked together and agreed on perfect peace among them for one night and morning.

Very slowly the sky paled. The youth failed to notice the bird arriving at the log, and the first sudden heart-beat startled him. There was his totem-bird, unconscious of being watched. Even so close at hand, the drumming had an eerie muffled quality, like the heart-beat in the body of the largest warrior.

Since it was not yet light enough to discern Drummer's every action, the motionless youth dared not risk alarming the sacred bird. When the sky became much brighter, he slowly, slowly raised his eyes among the old leaves, herbs, and ferns, to spy on the secretive bird in its spring ritual. Posturing on the resonant log, the male was addressing a small hen nearly hidden on the forest floor beyond. She was feigning indifference.

The lad's woods-trained eyes finally detected that the rolling drum-beat throbbed on *without* the wings striking the log, for the stiff moss-tips beneath the bird were unmoved. The first beats of a series were slow, and the short, rounded wings were thrusting forward, even somewhat upward, to flail against the sounding air. Soon the tempo picked up, and the wings were seen only as a vibrant blur. The Indian knew that Drummer, by beating forward against air, was tending to push himself backward, for the tensed tail was a prop to keep the bird from pitching over backward. And when the drumming whir suddenly ceased, the tail pressed the body quickly forward onto the log. Now the youth knew the secret of the heart-beat voice, heard so often resounding through the spring woods:

"Oomp! Oomp! Oomp! oom! oom, oom-oom-om-o-o-o-or-or-orroooom!

* * *

The vessels that landed in Vinland, Jamestown, Plymouth, and the southern shores were far in past time now, and a great university had been raised on the hill above the foot of Cayuga Lake, long before the Professor of Ornithology decided that no one really knew how the male Ruffed Grouse made its drumming sound.

Dr. Arthur A. Allen crept warily into his bird-blind, set up near a drumming log on massive Connecticut Hill. Dawn had not quite begun to lighten the east, and the season was still too early for insistent insect voices to make a leafy woods as noisy as a night nurse.

He had first erected the blind so far from the log that, while doubtless noted, it would not spook the sensitive birds. Over several days he had moved it closer and closer to the log, leaving it empty except for the glass lens from an old flashlight, fastened inside the camera hole to simulate a glinting lens. The grouse in the woods "accepted the blind" because it had not appeared suddenly and unexpectedly. Allen hoped to obtain a slow-motion sequence that would settle the bird's drumming technique beyond question. The professor had spent no small part of his life sitting in blinds, but never on such an important mission as he was on now.

From pre-dawn darkness he waited there, without coughing or sneezing. He was much farther from the log than the medicine youth had lain, but he had binoculars and a long-focus lens on a camera capable of both normal speed and slow-motion photography.

Not having spotted the skulking bird as it mounted the log, the scientist was startled by the first drum-beat. Since the light was far too dim to take pictures, he watched the grouse through binoculars and a slit in the fabric.

After a long period of intermittent drumming, the bird's behavior showed that a female had arrived and was waiting coyly beyond the decayed end of the log. After a few vicious pecks at the log beneath him, the cock grouse would drum vigorously. Then he would make a rush along the log toward the hen, peck the log masterfully, shake its head to fluff out the impressive purple ruff, then freeze in a pose revealing its spectacular, outspread tail-fan to the overwhelmed hen.

When the meter showed adequate illumination, Allen exposed a long sequence of the monochrome 35 mm. film for slow-motion projection, with the camera speeded up for more frames per second. If the two birds heard the whir of the camera shutter, it did not frighten or distract them from the business at hand.

Dr. Allen's movie showing and explanation caused quite a stir at the American Ornithologists Union meeting, and his paper was welcomed by the editor of the journal. To summarize his well-founded conclusions: (1) The drumming sound essentially does not result from wings striking the log or the bird's body; (2) the short, rounded wings beat not downward, but forward and slightly upward, at increasing tempo, ending in a blurred image even in slow-motion projection; and (3) pushing forward against the air pressed the body backward against the stiff, supporting tail; and (4) the bird recoiled forward as soon as the final flurry ended.

Thus was the mystery of the drumming phenomenon in the male *Bonasa umbellus* finally solved.

3

CHIEF POKAGON AND THE "GREEN MANSIONS" OF OLD INDIANA

THE site where Chicago now stands, "the place of the wild onions, or skunks," was included in the million acres "bought" from Chief Leopold Pokagon and his Potawatomi tribe. Leopold was a follower of Jesuit teachings and brought up his children in Christian piety. His son, later to become Chief Simon Pokagon, was ten years old when his father died and thirteen before he learned to speak any tongue except Algonquin, a language of 20,000 basic words. In later youth, Simon attended Notre Dame University and Oberlin College, proving a fine student in Greek and Latin. As chief of his tribe, he was a gifted orator and writer, the best-educated and most distinguished full-blooded American Indian of his day. His speech at the World's Fair of 1893, delivered on land formerly his tribe's property and not paid for, was the main attraction of Chicago Day. Simon wrote many articles printed in *Harpers*, *Review of Reviews*, etc., two remarkable books, and was a guest of Presidents Lincoln and Grant at their invitations. Yet he lived in a wigwam in northern Indiana in the traditional hunting-gathering style of his people, hard-pressed to gain a livelihood in the new world of the white man, because the remarkable woman he loved, Lonidaw, was not pleased with our civilization.

Simon wrote his life story and the one romance of his extraordinary life as a tragic prose-poem, in a quaint style which fitted the popular taste of the time before the turn of the century. Not the least of its charms is its authenticity. He declined offers to have the autobiography published in Chicago; it was brought out near his home where the whites and Indians knew him well and vouched for its truth. The direct quotations herein were taken from Simon's romantic old book.

On completion of his classical education, Simon returned to his natural life of hunting and fishing in northern Indiana and southern Michigan. There from time to time he glimpsed a shy and elusive young Indian girl, always accompanied and guarded by a white buck deer. Even the antlers were snow white. The girl and her mother lived in the only wigwam in a valley. They had escaped the roundup by white soldiers during the eviction from Potawatomi lands which the government falsely claimed had just been purchased from the tribe. The mother had fled into a swamp, and had given birth to the daughter alone in the shelter of a hollow sycamore, where she spent a week.

The mother told Simon thus about her daughter's uncanny vocal powers:

I often think the circumstances under which she was born in the swamp, amid the screams of birds of prey, and the cries of beasts, and songs of singing birds, had much to do with her wonderful gifts. She can imitate all creatures from the mouse to the elk, from the bee to the swan.

Lonidaw's father had been caught and forced to walk to an Indian reservation in a western state, and died of alcoholism. The Ottawas taught Kobunda and Lonidaw to do braid and bark work; the two camped near a lakeshore where suitable fiber-plants grew, tying bundles of them to the deer's antlers for carrying them home. Once, the smiling girl showed Simon how she could call down passenger pigeons to light on her head and shoulders, and by the hundreds on the ground close around her, as she voiced the musical chattering by which these birds herald their discovery of salty ground or a salt spring. Eventually, she gave Simon her explanation of her ability to speak in wild voices:

> The first thing I remember in early girlhood is of being delighted in the songs of birds . . . When older grown, I stole away from my mother to find the sources whence they came. A robin just above me poured forth its joyful song of praise. . . . Unconsciously I too began to sing its song, and in after years, when mating birds each other wooed, I sang with them; when awakened by alarm, I joined with them in their shrill and startling cries; when assailed by birds of prey, I joined with them in their shout of defiance; when the nests were robbed, I joined them in their bitter moans; when their young abandoned their nests and flew away, I joined them in their plaintive chirps to call them back; when their companions were lost, I sang with them the funeral dirge. And so it was I learned to mourn and to rejoice with them, and grew in sympathy with all the tenants of the woods.

In spring Lonidaw often wore a crown of her favorite flower, Trailing Arbutus, and wove wreaths of other wildflowers for her pet deer to wear around its neck. The Indians of the region considered albino deer as sacred, exempt from being hunted. When Lonidaw saved the newborn white fawn from starvation, it became imprinted on the girl as its mother, and grew up to protect her like a guard dog. Simon described the two at play.

> The deer would run in circles swift about her, then turning square about, rush straight toward her, dropping on his knees in front of her, and rubbing his chin on the ground by a rolling motion to and fro with his neck and head; then, like a purring cat, roll over, and springing to his feet, like a young dog would run round and round the old wigwam, stopping just in sight now and then, as if trying to play hide-and-seek with her. At last he walked boldly up to her, and she placed her arm over his neck and shoul-

ders, patting him under the neck and chin, which he seemed to enjoy, with eyes half-closed as if almost asleep. I will not admit that I was jealous of the deer, but most humbly confess that I *did* covet the attention he received.

Soon the snow-white animal sensed that the threat of his antlers and front hooves, effective against other men, would not keep Simon away from Lonidaw. When Simon proposed that she marry him in the native manner, and the girl and her mother agreed, it was in the season when the buck had no antlers. Lonidaw cautioned Simon that they must now teach the pet to control his jealous heart, and they walked hand in hand toward the sacred animal. "He shook his head, stopped a few feet away, there a moment stood, then turned around facing us with the most forlorn look I ever beheld . . . and walked sullenly away." Although he had always lived close to the wigwam, he was never seen again.

The lovers were married, and lived in a wigwam by a lake. "Happy in each other's love, we floated down life's stream, all unprepared for the cataracts and rocks along the shore." Lonidaw planted wildflowers all along the trail leading to their home, and trained her dog Zowan to collect white water lilies from the lake and bring to them. The first child was the boy O-lon-daw, the second a daughter much like Lonidaw, named Hazel Eyes.

Was the fictional Rima in British ornithologist W. H. Hudson's subsequent novel *Green Mansions* (1904) inspired by the real-life Lonidaw? Hudson's white bird-woman of the Argentine rain forest was finally done in by Indians; the Pokagons were North American Indians subjected to horrendous abuse at the hands of whites. The whole family save Chief Simon was lost through the white man and his whiskey directly or indirectly, even though only Lonidaw's father and son succumbed to the "devil in a jug." Simon's slim, lovely "queen of the woods" was only thirty-five when she drowned attempting to rescue her drowned daughter whom drunken white men in a boat had run down. The dog Zowan, on his own, brought white lilies from the lake and covered her fresh grave. Simon continued to live in his lonely wigwam, finding his only consolation in Nature and his strong Christian faith.

His book *Queen of the Woods* sensitively reflects a profound love of all life, and, coming from the heart and mind of a full-blooded American native, touchingly attests to the line in Longfellow's *Hiawatha*—"Every human heart is human." Today, Pokagon State Park in northeastern Indiana preserves a remnant of the sort of lands and waters and their living things that the Pokagons knew so well. Also, a twenty-five acre tract in Noble County, dedicated as the Lonidaw Nature Preserve, contains a small lake and perpetuates "the spirit of the woods," said to be the meaning of the name Lonidaw.

4

SKY, LAND, AND THE POLYGON PRINCIPLE

The six-sided figure is a recurrent theme of our experience and our mental constructs of both the atmosphere and the earth. Far more of the beauty and interest of Nature, beyond the sky effects based on hexagonal ice-crystals, is attributable to the geometry of polygons.

Basic to organic compounds is the graphic formula with six carbon atoms, a hexagon of connected atoms termed the "benzene ring." This molecular hexagon is not seen through our retinas except when represented on paper or blackboard, but is clearly seen by the mind's eye of chemists in Nature and on their laboratory shelves.

Even though nothing is more individual in detail than an atmospheric aggregation of frozen water in crystalline form, each snowflake is a hexagon with six sides or points. This form is the inevitable consequence of a water molecule's structure, and water is so prevalent that our planet should have been named "Oceanus."

Among the more impalpable expressions of the "six-pack" idea in the atmosphere is a round-figure level of wind chill. When the winter wind blows at fifty miles an hour with an air temperature of a degree below zero Fahrenheit, the damaging effect on exposed human flesh is *sixfold* what it would be at that same temperature in a dead calm. This combination of intensities of two atmospheric elements well illustrates the importance of the wind chill factor. Yet science had not understood or systematized this effect of weather on people until 1945.

The most accurate and useful concept of world life zones was made known two decades ago by ecologist Leslie Holdridge. His model is depicted on paper by a three-axis graph. The gradient on each axis is expressed logarithmically on the base 2, the values doubling and redoubling. The axes represent average total annual biotemperature (months with means below freezing are omitted), average total annual precipitation, and the potential evapotranspiration/precipitation ratio. Because the chart is built on three axes, each resulting unit, called life zone or plant formation, delimited by the value-lines forms a *hexagon*, equally weighted and of equal size on the paper to all other hexagons. There are 116 of these life zones generally found on the Earth. They are defined climatically rather than geographically, hence do not conform with ordinary world maps. The model, then, appears as a honeycomb of hexagons, each cell of which represents a distinct life zone. On a map of the actual continents, the theoretical hexagonal units will not appear as hexagons but as areas of varying sizes and shapes which show the land surfaces occupied by those climatic types.

On a life zone map of the United States, the life zone covering the largest area (about one-fifth of the contiguous U.S.) is that in the southeastern region from Indianapolis southward and Tulsa eastward (except the south half of peninsular Florida.) The climate of this Warm Temperate Moist Forest life zone covers a roughly rectangular portion of the nation.

The six-legged or hexapodal group we term Insecta sees the world through relatively huge compound eyes, each eye consisting of hundreds of tiny columnar hexagons. Honeycombs are hexagonal.

Turning from the atmosphere and living things to rocks and soil, we find six fundamental forms which chemicals take in crystalizing. Common or garden variety mud seems as amorphous a substance as anything that comes readily to mind, but on drying it shrinks to form roughly hexagonal surface plates or flakes.

Tremendously larger hexagons, pentagons, and squares are formed in wet arctic and sub-arctic soils, not by drying but by freezing. In summer these "soil polygons" are familiar features on airphotos of far northern country. They are among the many and fascinating landscape forms that accompany permafrost, perennially frozen ground, which experts map as occurring in one-fifth of North America. Two clearly distinct types of polygons are (1) raised-center polygons, with water in the surrounding moat-like trough that separates each from its neighbors, and (2) depressed-center polygons, in which the moats are replaced by dry ridges and the inner low portions are usually ponded.

The Palisades of the Hudson, extending for twenty five miles in New York and New Jersey, are hexagonal or pentagonal columns of igneous rock seen by more people than any other. Similar formations are well known at Devil's Tower, Wyoming, and Devils's Postpile in California, and less spectacular displays are seen at Mount Rainier, the Olympic Peninsula, and many other areas of volcanism. The joints or cracks which separate the massive columns were caused by shrinkage-pull as the molten rock was cooling and solidifying. The pattern formed by the network of narrow cracks is more or less hexagonal or pentagonal in cross section.

As at the famous Palisades of the Hudson, and at the riverside cliffs of the upper Columbia, we commonly see the exposed edge of the igneous rock deposit, which shows the rock prisms lengthwise. On remote Et Then Island in Great Slave Lake, Canada, however, one can climb up one of the natural ramps between the cliffs and come out upon the barren rock of the great flat sill of diorite that forms the plateau capping the island. To form this sill, an intrusion of molten rock was forced upward, spread out laterally well below the earth's surface, and cooled very slowly to form unusually large columns. While botanizing on this plateau, I climbed to the top of a projecting rock prism (Chapter headpiece illustration) that stood sixteen feet above the general surface. The top of this column measured eleven feet across its hexagonal top. I surmounted it easily because it was the central, tallest shaft among a cluster of columns that extended upward stepwise toward it.

The flat top of each of these columns, now varying in height, had originally been at the same level as the general surface of the plateau, since the level was uniform throughout just after the sill cooled and was exposed by erosion. Soon near-incredible change began in the wide, flat surface. Water would seep into the joints in summer, and each winter it would freeze at least once. One of the curious properties of water is that it expands when it freezes. Very, very slowly the expansion of minute sheets of freezing water levered the long heavy columns inexorably upward. Perhaps it was a "net" rise, since there may have been some falling back into the hole occasionally. But a column was so close-packed within its cavity that it was wedged upward during at least eight thousand years by alternate freezing and thawing. In the case of the highest prism, from which I was "monarch of all I surveyed," the change of sixteen feet in that time was remarkable. The elements that had successfully defied gravity and differentiated the formerly featureless plateau surface were simple ones—water, temperature changes, and especially Time.

The prevalence of hexagons of these kinds and others suggests some thoughts on the nature of Nature, since hexagons are both mathematical and aesthetic, economical of material and space, and, above all, integrative and synthesizing. They illustrate one familiar way in which the world is "put together."

5

TWO AMATEUR NATURALISTS WHO INVENTED THE TWENTIETH CENTURY

HENRY Ford's hobbies were history and natural history. Like many amateur naturalists, Ford was active in promoting conservation legislation. The Audubon Society and C. Hart Merriam's federal Biological Survey wrote a bill for protecting migratory birds and Ford helped get it through the Congress.

Ford brought Seton and Burroughs to Washington for a week, paying all expenses. In enlisting them for this lobbying effort, he told each, "There are only two naturalists in the United States that every Senator will come out into the lobby to discuss such matters with—John Burroughs and Thompson Seton." The latter said later that he had to do all the talking, but the bill passed, forming the basis for treaty protection among Canada, Mexico and the United States.

Burroughs showed Seton around Washington, since he

knew the city and had there written his first nature book, *Wake Robin*.

Ford was younger than Thomas Alva Edison and looked to him as his mentor as well as close friend. They had adjoining winter estates in Fort Myers, Florida, and frequently entertained John Burroughs there. For many years these three and Harvey Firestone took Ford cars out on long tent-camping vacations, on which Burroughs served as private naturalist for the party in camp and on the road. Burroughs was not technically inclined, not only in comparison with his technological-giant friends, but compared with nearly anyone. Once, against his better judgment, he accepted the gift of a Model-T Ford from its inventor. John O'Birds was afraid of the car. One day he drove it out of his barn at Woodchuck Lodge, not through the door as he intended, but through the side of the barn.

Edison invented the use of royal palm trees for street and estate planting. He had the collectors for his extensive botanical garden around his Fort Myers home bring in a number of these stately trees from tropical wilds and plant them in the city. These were later distributed until today their concrete-like columns line streets of many towns in southern Florida. The old house, botanical garden, and laboratory are popular tourist attractions today.

Thomas Edison was interested in plants both intrinsically and for their practical uses in his experiments. He tried the fibers of many plants from his gardens as possible filaments for his incandescent light bulbs, and their thorns for his phonograph needles. He worked extensively on methods of extracting rubber from the latex of various wild plants, including goldenrod.

Nature-lover Edison saw that his son Theodore was given instruction in natural history. Theodore wrote me that he does not know how he acquired his interest in Nature, because he cannot remember a time when he was not interested in it.

Father and Mother both loved Nature, and I grew up surrounded by a wide range of beautiful trees and other forms of natural life at our New Jersey and Florida homes. I carried out a lot of "experiments" on my own. For example, I remember that as a kid I spent many hours alone studying ants; to see how a scouting ant communicated with other ants to start a whole parade of ants to a piece of candy; to see how ants were able to follow a "trail" across a smooth surface; etc. . . . As I understand it, my father thought that life might be a fundamental component of the universe, which, like matter and energy, could be transformed in various ways but not created or destroyed. We are accustomed to think of ourselves as single entities, but father wondered if each so-called individual might not really be an organism engineered and operated by a whole society of more fundamental entities he called "monoids."

Biologists have shown recently that certain essential components of human cells were once separate micro-organisms, that they invaded the cells of beings ancestral to man and are now indispensible to the functioning of higher life forms like man. Another suggestive case is that of the distinctive nests of tropical termite species. It is quite mysterious what sort of control is exerted among these insects to insure that the colony of a given species can build a complex, towering nest in a characteristic pattern of internal structure which is just as indicative of the species taxonomy as are the physical traits of individual insect bodies. The nest represents an emergent integration on a higher level, each insect being one "monoid" within its colony.

Theodore Edison is an engineer who has been an environmental activist lifelong, particularly in the field of natural area preservation. He states in a letter, "Although my primary training was in applied physics, I am now spending most of my time on environmental problems. For many years

I have felt that we were making too much technical progress without paying enough attention to what we were doing to our environment and social relations." This closely parallels Charles A. Lindbergh's mature philosophy.

A neat point made in one of Edison's letters concerns the intrusion of artificialities and "developments" into even a small part of an outstanding natural area. This would be comparable, he wrote, to the addition of a black, indelible mustache to the Mona Lisa painting when the Louvre guard wasn't looking, though some might defend it on the ground that it covered only a small percentage of the painting. Also, it takes just one wailing infant at a concert or opera performance to spoil the whole aesthetic effect. I think his point answers the charge that preservationists are mere "elitists." If they are such, then everyone who opposes the added mustache on Ms. Lisa, or a brassiere on the Winged Victory statue, is also an elitist.

6

ORNITHEOLOGY

THE communicants of the popular faith, Ornitheology, of whom the writer is one, consider John James Audubon as the original prophet. His beatification began early. The 1862 book *National Portrait Gallery* appends this legend to the artist's portrait.

His long raven locks hung curling over his shoulders, yet unshorn from the wilderness . . . His fine-featured face bespoke a sort of wild independence; and then such an eye, keen as that of a falcon! His foreign accent and broken English speech . . . removed him still further out of the commonplace circle of this everyday world of ours, and his whole demeanor—it might be with us partly imagination—was colored to our thought by a character of conscious freedom and dignity, which he had habitually acquired in his long and lonely wandering among the woods, where he had lived in the uncompanioned love and delight of nature, and in the studious observation of all the ways of her winged children.

The combination of "Aud" with "bon" conjures up the good sounds of bird song in the lost, wild America of a bygone time. His is undoubtedly the best known name among the early zoological explorers of this continent. Some portion of his present renown is doubtless due to the National Audubon Society and its excellent magazine *Audubon*. This organization is most fortunate that his name was not John J. Smith. His last name is distinctive as well as distinguished. Who knows any other Audubon? No individual with that surname is listed in the Manhattan or Greater Washington telephone directories. The man was as different as his name, as graceful and colorful as his cherished paintings. His image was to some degree the product of artful cultivation, as when he wore frontier buckskins in the drawing rooms of London and Edinburgh. But Nature had provided him with a fine start toward a glamorous reputation.

Audubon, of course, was much more of an artist than a technical ornithologist. He described as new to science the magnificent Great White Heron of Florida Bay and the Keys. It seems a pity that the naturalist has lost this distinction, in that the American Ornithologists' Union in 1973 demoted it to a subspecies with the Great Blue Heron, leaving the vernacular name unchanged for the white "color morph." The situation in this polymorphic species group is much more complex and uncertain than with bird species in general, and so much more genetic work is needed that the present nomenclature is not necessarily final.

While working on the splendid wading birds of southern Florida, Audubon was in his element. By this time he had learned to draw bills and feet accurately. The best site he found for field collecting was Sandy Key, now in Everglades National Park. In his day there were about two million of these native birds where today there are twenty thousand.

Audubon painted many of his Florida bird portraits in a small, second-story room of Geiger (or Audubon) House in Key West, now an Audubon museum. In that room we were privileged to inspect the four volumes of his double-elephant folio, *Birds of America*. Soon after, the set was stolen from there, but recovered later. Of the less than 200 complete sets produced, about 130 are known today. Each one of them in decent condition is valued at one million dollars.

It seems doubtful that any person less industrious, charming, gifted, and self-confident than Audubon could have succeeded, in the sophisticated and critical culture of Britain, with such an expensive project based on the bird life of a foreign country. It would have been impossible without the tutoring income of his wife Lucy, the daughter of a rich English neighbor at Audubon's first home in America, now near Audubon, Pennsylvania. She was a true patroness of art and science through her work in holding their family together. One of her later pupils was the young George Bird Grinnell, who founded the first Audubon Society in 1886.

Many of Audubon's successors, starting with Louis Agassiz Fuertes, have painted birds more artistically and more true to life, but Audubon is still the only bird artist most people can name, and this is unlikely to change.

* * *

"Bird-watching" is now a favorite outdoor sport of millions. During my years of working for a doctorate at Cornell University with a minor in ornithology with Professor A.A. Allen, and during the summer of 1937 when I taught botany at the first Audubon Nature Camp in its second season, I never heard the term. It is a British term that our public has adopted more recently. Researchers in bird behavior really watch them; amateur birders merely identify them, by and large, and keep lists. Some of them are pretty competitive about it. One recently attempted to find eight hundred species in one year, and very nearly reached that count in a photo-finish.

Bird-watching or hunting and fishing, which some consider antithetical, offer the usual approaches toward an eventual broad and mature interest in Nature. After one of these interests has developed in a person or an organization, the next logical steps are belief and action in conservation-preservation of ecosystems, not merely particular species or groups of plants or animals. Most of the large, effective outdoor groups followed this course during their histories, having started from a less sophisticated, more special interest.

The National Audubon Society, in the late Thirties under John Baker, was decades ahead of general public perception in its stress on the web of life. Ecologist William Vogt edited *Bird Lore*, the precursor of *Audubon*, and in 1938 he first published Aldo Leopold's historic essay which later formed the acme of that author's influential 1949 book *Sand County Almanac*. Although the public considers Leopold as a literary naturalist and outdoor philosopher, he was basically a scientist who served as president of the professional Ecological Society of America.

Just before the Wall Street crash of '29 which initiated the Great Depression, a wealthy importer who lacked formal education but not financial savvy sold his seat on the New York Stock Exchange. Albert Brand then retired and moved with his family to Ithaca. He began a long period of years in which he financed Professor Allen and his assistants in pioneering the field recording of bird songs and sounds. I occasionally assisted in the sound truck as a volunteer. Support and personal work by Brand contributed greatly to building up the Cornell Laboratory of Ornithology with its Sapsucker Woods station, later assisted by another major private donor. Until Allen's retirement his office was graced by a mounted Emperor Penguin which I had brought back from Antarctica to give my old professor.

Aldo Leopold, the father of game management, started out in forestry. While a federal forester in Albuquerque he became an avid duck hunter. Thus, he became familiar with a rare representative of the mallard complex, the New Mexican Duck, which inhabited the middle and lower Rio Grande Valley. At that time and much later, no one had reported finding the nest of this subspecies of the Mexican Duck.

At the time I lived in Albuquerque in the mid-Forties, this was almost the last undiscovered nest of any United States species of bird. Bird scientists were as eager to get an original nest finding into the literature as amateurs were to log an extensive life list. Artist George Miksch Sutton, who was also a Cornell graduate student and instructor when I was, had recently described the first nest of the Harris Sparrow from Churchill, Manitoba. No nest of the Coppery Trogon had been found in the United States. The nest of the New Mexican Duck was still unreported when I went to teach in Albuquerque.

To abbreviate a long story, I finally in 1945 found several nests of breeding pairs in the Cienaga (Marsh) of San Simone in extreme southwestern New Mexico, described the egg from twenty-three mostly uncollected specimens, and spent a summer working out the ecological life history. Thus, the first description of the bird's breeding habits was published in *"The Auk."*

Taxonomy, the non-exact science of classification, is partly art. Workers in this field tend to fall within two groups, "splitters" and "lumpers." The latter have a taste for larger, more inclusive species. The splitter, putting more emphasis on differences than on similarities, prefers more species, each more narrowly defined. At different times, one or the other attitude may be more in fashion among systematists.

At the time of my study, the New Mexican was a subspecies with the Mexican Duck. Some years later, through a lumping decision, this distinction was eliminated and my birds became Mexican Ducks, as their relatives in Mexico had been all along. Thus, the bird I worked on, already rare, was, shall we say, exterminated by a stroke of the pen? This cost me my record as the finder of a new nest—one of the very last to be found in our nation. But as a part-time, almost amateur ornithologist, I took this philosophically. Since the same sort of misfortune befell the great Audubon, why should lesser mortals be immune?

In biological classification, distinctions are man-made. Nature, over time, has woven a seamless web of life. What man has done on paper, man can reverse on paper. The New Mexican Duck may someday fly again.

7

WILD BIRD ANTICS

IN the lonely, jumbled ice-wilderness in the Bay of Whales, only the distant trumpeting of an Emperor Penguin is heard above the wind as it moans among the bizarre pinnacles. The strange, reedy cry aptly expresses the spirit of this remote solitude never intended for man or his sledge-dogs.

Besides my expedition job studying life histories of two seal species, collecting their skins, skulls, and embryos, and collecting and preparing skins of oceanic birds through the nineteen months, I was asked to capture nineteen living Emperors to be kept alive by sailor friends for the Brookfield Zoo, Chicago. To catch these large and powerful birds is the least of it. The men assigned to care for them enroute home had to feed them forcibly with strips of thawed fish, which had been shipped frozen from New Zealand. In this ordeal, two men were needed to a bird. At the end of two months, one of the Emperors had progressed so far that he would open his mouth for food. Others acquired this talent later on, but none ever learned to pick up food.

The pupils of penguin eyes must open wide enough for vision in dimly lit water, often beneath sea-ice, and to see something in the winter darkness when Emperors breed. But the iris must close down the pupil drastically during bright days out of water in the summer. The close acquaintance we enjoyed with penguins enabled me to publish a fact no one had noted before—that the Emperor eye, when closed to a dot-like pupil only a millimeter across, has this light-gathering aperture not round but diamond shaped, with four sharp corners.

Aboard ship and heading for the Galapagos in the southern autumn, these Emperors and twenty-one Adelie Penguins were housed in an air-conditioned, refrigerated room forty feet long, with a swimming pool. Daily, each bird had to be promenaded on deck to dry its plumage. Friction of the stiff tail-feathers against the iron deck-plates wore their tails down to a stub without tail feathers. After the Emperors died from a lung-fungus infection in the zoo, the eight best ones were mounted for a habitat group at Field Museum, now the Chicago Museum of Natural History. In this display, the mounted birds all face the observer so that he or she will not notice the damaged tails. Only the painted birds on the backdrop reveal their back sides.

Although the Bay is four hundred miles from the nearest penguin rookery, the piratical Antarctic Skua was with us commonly all summer. When I was still naive about the taking ways of Skua gulls, I left several seal embryos lying out on the sledge, and the skuas made off with them when my back was turned. (Skulls and embryos were by-products of killing seals for dog food.) But one day their thieving propensity was helpful to us biologists. We were dynamiting off the edge of the sea-ice for unusual fish specimens. The killed fish would float to the surface, but a current coming from beneath the ice carried them out to sea northward, and we had no boat. The Skua gulls would retrieve them from the water, fly to solid ice where we were, and alight to eat them. We would then charge yelling at the birds to scare them from their booty, and add it to our collection.

Though Skuas, like all Antarctic birds, depend on the surrounding ocean for food, there is evidence that individual Skuas may have flown across the 10,000-foot high polar plateau, at least 2,100 hungry miles from the Weddell Sea to the Ross Sea.

Only two of the seventeen species of penguin are truly Antarctic in distribution, and one species is confined to the Galapagos Archipelago, where some of them breed right on the Equator, a tropical rather than polar penguin. When we returned homeward by way of these islands, we observed some of these diminutive fellows in the black lava caverns opening to the sea along the edge of Albemarle Island. At Admiral Byrd's request, we launched the motor sailor from the flagship deck, risked the heaving surf within one jagged, shallow cave, and managed to capture one Galapagos Penguin. This job was not (in one of the leader's favorite expressions) "All for Science." This penguin was desired to reap unusual publicity for another Byrd.

Although the bird did not seem to be a young one, it somehow became imprinted on, or at least attached to the Admiral. It did not mix with the common penguin people in the tank-room 'tween decks, but lived in style in the Admiral's quarters on the bridge. And it would follow Byrd around, at his heels like a pet dog. Each publicity photo implied a wordplay on Byrd's name. I think this sprightly little clown found a home at Brookfield Zoo after we reached the states.

While writing this, I glance up occasionally to check on a minor mystery outside my study window. A solitary Cedar Waxwing stands watch on the topmost point of a Scotch pine tree. It has been there all day, practically, for five days now, but leaves for the night's roosting. Is it moulting now in late August? Birds often skulk in hiding during the moult; this one is inactive but far from hidden, and we have not seen it abandon its post to seek food. Nor is it doing the familiar fly-catcher act, of swooping from his perch to catch passing insects from the air.

It was when I was ten that bird life first touched my feelings. My friends and I had dedicated our leisure time to reducing the English Sparrow peril. Automobiles were catching on, but horses were still common enough to support a large, verminous population of "sputzies." We trapped them by arranging four loose bricks on the ground and baiting a hollow among them with cracked corn. An upper, tilted brick was held up by a trigger mechanism of twigs; when the bird disturbed this, it was caught in the cavity and appropriately disposed of.

My last adventure as a sparrow trapper made quite an impression on me. On approaching the trap which I maintained in a brushy ravine in town, I noted with the usual excitement that the top brick was down. Then—a shocking horror! The hollow contained a male Cardinal, its skull cracked by the falling brick. My gang had not thought that any real bird would fall for such crude devices. The guilt and revulsion I felt while burying the lovely creature reduced my youthful barbarity.

Probably few bird-lovers can cite the exact incident that made them that way. At age twelve, I was waiting for a pal beneath a small maple tree on a hilltop at the edge of town. I became aware of the lisping of some secretive little birds among the half-grown leaves. They retreated from my approach. To see them at close range, I climbed into the dense crown of branches. Once in the tree, I was apparently accepted, perhaps as another bird, by creatures I had not seen or imagined until that day.

Smaller than any bird I knew except hummingbirds, they flitted about me without indication of fear, cocking bold, inquisitive black eyes at me. I thought them incredibly smooth and well-groomed, very self-assured and at home among the young leaves. Their neat color pattern made them perfect jewels, proudly alive in showing off their rare beauty. The male's favorite pose, with wings slightly drooped and tail elevated, gave him a very smart, bantam-like appearance.

Back home, I consulted Mother's copy of *Bird Neighbors* by Neltje Blanchan, and learned that the subjects of my quiet watch were Chestnut-sided Warblers. John Burroughs had written in his *Wake Robin*, "He is one of the rarest and handsomest of the warblers; his white breast and throat, chestnut sides, and yellow crown show conspicuously. But little is known of his habits or haunts."

The next wood warblers I saw were also sharing tree-crowns with me in the tall hemlocks holding up my high tree-platform at our family camp in the Laurel Ridge of Pennsylvania. The Black-throated Blue Warblers also came within arm's reach fearlessly. The crisp, sharply limned plumage and the sure and efficient actions of these mites convinced me that Burroughs had written truly that "The most precious things in life have no commercial value."

One summer day I trudged barefoot along the dusty roads from our mountain cabin down toward a familiar fishing-hole in Loyalhanna Creek. As I walked past the old barn of a farmstead, a flock of chittering Barn Swallows began swooping in force to within a few feet of my head. I was somewhat alarmed by their attentions, but even more puzzled.

It was not until I passed the barn on my return, hours later, that the explanation came to me, during the repitition of the strange behavior. My tubular steel fishing rod was now telescoped down to a length of three feet, and carried over my shoulder. Dangling from its tip on an inconspicuous gut leader was a gray hackle trout fly. The swallows had not been interested in me, pro or con. They were after that artificial fly. Fortunately, none was quite bold enough to catch it and be caught.

A decade later, another masterful flyer also proved exciting, though seen at a greater distance. Duck Hawks in arrow-like flight to and from their cliff eyrie beside Taughannock Falls thundering toward Cayuga Lake were obvious monarchs of their world. Had anyone tried to tell me that the eastern genotype of the swift and terrible Peregrine Falcon would be completely exterminated by man in less than three decades, I'd have replied that a pair of them had always nested in the mist of Taughannock, and always would.

Beyond the south end of Cayuga Lake looms the mountain modestly termed Connecticut Hill, a chief site of the state conservation department's long and thorough study of the Ruffed Grouse population. I was one of the graduate students employed each Saturday in the survey crew; an assistant cruised with me from early autumn to late spring. In winter, snowshoes kept us over the deep drifts. We saw some of the grouse, heard more, and traced the sign and activities of many. In the awakening woods of early spring, their drumming was the characteristic sound. When one's unwary step scattered a family of downy young and they again froze motionless, it was virtually impossible to see one unless it ran again. One never grows accustomed to the explosive burst of an adult Ruffed Grouse as it shatters the air in taking off at one's feet.

Also working for a Cornell doctorate then were George Miksch Sutton and Olin Sewall Pettingill. Artist-ornithologist-writer Sutton related amusingly the account of the first discovery of the Harris Sparrow's nest. He took his small team to Churchill, Manitoba, where he calculated they *should* be nesting. A rival party from England was also there looking for the same unknown nest. The search reached a high pitch of competition and excitement.

One day George was watching the movements of a female Harris Sparrow, when it alighted on an empty wooden box someone had discarded on the tundra. Painted in bold, black letters just beneath the perching bird was the trade name of the product it had contained—"HARRIS." The sight gave George a glow of premonition. He felt sure that he would find the nest that day.

The bird flew from the tell-tale box to a clump of low vegetation on the ground. When Sutton went over and flushed the bird, there was the first nest of the Harris Sparrow known to science!

In southern New Mexico, my detailed investigation of the rare and exceptionally shy New Mexican Duck brought two curious antics to light. Through field glasses, I saw a female lay one egg on a bare, dry mudflat, and abandon it at once and for good. Another female nesting in a normal marshy area where I had found the first known nest of the species, flew up from a nest as I cautiously approached. I was shocked to see that she was carrying an egg in her beak, and that soon the shell broke and an embryo dangled from the female's bill. Later I read that Mallards also carry off their eggs on occasion.

While my wife and I were hiking the Klapatche area at Mount Rainier, a small flock of Gray Jays approached us, their calls soliciting a handout although we had no food in evidence. The boldest one landed on the crown of my straw hat. I was not able to unlimber the camera before he departed, but I clapped the hat on Elizabeth's head, and focused the camera on it. Just then one of the Camp Robber birds again alighted on the hat, posed pertly long enough for me to photograph it, and flew at the sound of the shutter. Although Gray Jays sometimes swoop down and snatch frying bacon from the pan, we had never known a strange jay to perch on a person. More recently, Florida Jays did so while being fed nuts.

Just now I have, temporarily, a long grizzled beard in order to impersonate Oom John (as his friend Teddy Roosevelt called him) in my slide talk "The Return of John Burroughs and His Literary Naturalist Friends." This beard is literally "for the birds." Just after giving my final show, I shall clip off the beard, save it until the chipping sparrows and other hair-raising birds are nest-building, and see what use they make of it.

In 1816, within a few days of Indiana statehood, Tom Lincoln brought his family from Kentucky into southern Indiana. Abraham was almost eight, and he lived there near Little Pigeon Creek in Spencer County until he was twenty-one. The President tells in his autobiography that while the cabin walls were not yet caulked his parents left him alone for a time, a loaded gun at hand for protection. A flock of burnished Wild Turkeys strutted into the clearing. Abe thrust the gun barrel through a crack between the logs, and shot one of them. The bloody mutilation and death throes of the once-splendid fowl distressed the boy so much that he determined never to kill any game again, and kept this resolve throughout life.

John Burroughs, as a much older boy, once stalked a flock of Passenger Pigeons on the farm in the Catskills. The rolling motion of the stupendous flock, its roar and turmoil so intimidated and bemused him that he forgot what he had come out for. The gun went undischarged, although one easy shot might have brought down scores of the succulent birds.

I have seen no live Passenger Pigeons, but I have some remote, if sad, pleasure in knowing that the last wild flock was still in existence during at least the first two weeks of my life. My most thrilling bird observation was an unexpected, close view of a magnificent male Quetzal flying, its spectacular tail in tow, across a clearing in the Costa Rican rain forest. I could understand how the Mayans could worship such a bird, and permit only their chiefs to wear its plumes. The sight of my one Quetzal fulfilled the implicit promise made to me many years before by my first wood warbler.

8

NATURE'S BONSAI

IT is said that character in man stems from struggles against adversity. It certainly does in the case of trees. A Japanese horticultural artist gives a little tree a hard time, molding from its stressful life the picturesque bonsai. Such a cultured tree is too aristocratic to be useful in commonplace ways. It does not produce lumber, shade, or pulpwood, only wonder and beauty.

Like these man-made bonsai, the trees that I call natural bonsai are severely stunted but very long-lived. We need not expect to find them on normal, favorable woodland sites. In places too rigorous for sensible trees to live, these trees gesticulate agonizingly on the lunatic fringes of tree distribution. Their habitats are too cold, or waterless, or rocky, or windy to support trees that attract men in their insatiable search for utility.

California contains, among other superlatives, the

world's oldest living trees. These are not the giant sequoias, as was so long believéd. The bristle-cone pines, some of which have lived more than four thousand and six hundred years, attain but a small fraction of the height of the justly-named big tree. In the case of many ancient survivors in the White Mountains, they are hardly twice the height of a man, and their strange, bottle-brush foliage is extremely sparse. Often the few living branches from the squat, massive trunk connect vitally with earth only by way of one narrow remaining strip of bark snaking up the otherwise dead trunk. There only, outer dead bark protects the thin ribbon of life in inner bark and outermost wood of the elephantine trunk. One special living bristle-cone pine there is the world's oldest living thing, even though its inner portions have not lived for millennia. The only living wood, what very little there is of it, is quite modern and superficial. As in other bonsai-like trees wild or domesticated, fragility runs parallel with longevity. Like a human centenarian, its form and function expresses toughness by age alone, merely by not having succumbed to death.

Ponderosa or western yellow pine is common, though scattered, at middle elevations of the extensive New Mexican lava bed along the continental divide near Grants, the "uranium city." The trees, rooted in narrow joints and crevices in the sun-heated, black rock, seldom exceed a dozen feet regardless of age, and appear artistically distorted in form. The great average longevity of these stunted trees first becomes obvious when one notices that both seedlings and old, dead individuals are practically nonexistent.

One twist-stemmed veteran I photographed reached upward only six feet. Three decades later, I found it dead and decayed away except for the basal two feet that projected from a dome-shaped burl, also dead, that spread over the lava just above the hair-line crack which the roots had penetrated. A saw, sandpaper, and twelve-power lens revealed the life story in a cross-section of the trunk a foot above the basal burl. This slender stem had taken, on the average, ninety-two years to produce *each inch* of growth in diameter. The tree had survived near-intolerable rigors for 220 years; it was much older than the tall, normal ponderosa pines on decent soil away from the lava bed. As with a certain group of peasants in the eastern Caucasus, an extreme life span furnishes compensation for a slowed and strictured rate of living. These lives, men and trees, are thinned and attenuated, like the rubber of a stretched band.

Comparing my subalpine fir photos taken at Mount Rainier's timberline with the same actual trees thirty-three years later, I found very little, and in some cases no, growth or difference recognizable externally. However, for this thin green line of heroes storming the rocky snowbound slopes, surrender would mean death. Each summer must bring some growth, even though the new wood may be of only microscopic width and discontinuous over the tree.

Somewhat below timberline in the northern Rockies, but at the highest elevations where extensive closed forests of evergreens can grow, the trees stand erect, with normal straight form as seen in life. However, killed by forest fires and standing for decades without bark, the trees show grain in the wood running around and up at a forty-five degree angle, often. The new wood had been originally laid down, not vertically as in a normal tree, but in a spirally-twisted orientation which is quite hidden as long as the bark covers the wood. This orientation of the elongated wood cells is not caused by wind, but by a combination of factors on and in the ground. The rockier, steeper, and more infertile the mountainside, the tighter is the spiral of grain formed by the tracheid cells. The most extreme cases of this sort are found on high lava beds where there is enough precipitation for Douglas firs but essentially no soil. Some weathered, dead fir trunks there have such a flat spiral in the exposed wood that the grain in places runs practically horizontally around the trunk. In life, when much of the sparse water obtained by the roots has to revolve round and round the trunk on its delayed course upward to the leaves, no wonder such a tree that is two feet in trunk diameter is able to grow only twenty-five feet tall.

The lives of artificial and natural bonsai drive home one point more forcefully than normal trees on ordinary sites — the girth and height of the individual tree may give little indication of its actual age. The hereditary potential in terms of growth rate is strongly influenced for good or ill by the tree's immediate environment, made up of many different factors. For example, in the richest woods of sugar maple, a shade-tolerant species, a spindling young maple only an inch in diameter can be a quarter-century old. After the fall of the veterans that shaded it, such a young-looking tree begins rapid growth. The foresters call this being "released."

At alpine timberlines, constraints on growth and survival are mostly physical ones; in bogs and other peatlands they are more likely to be chemical factors. In an extreme type of Adirondack acid-bog, one finds a curious contradiction. The red spruce trees *apparently* grade down to younger ages, the closer one approaches the central open water and gets farther from the tall, parent trees in the surrounding mature timber. Is it not reasonable that small, young trees are invading the bog mat to nearer and nearer the edge of the central open pond as the latter fills in with time's passage? This apparent gradient is deceptive; it is true only of tree size. Ring counts tell the real story. There is no gradation of age. The apparent seedlings of the waterside are actually as old as the tall spruce in the drier forest nearby.

The six-inch-tall red spruce in the youngest part of the bog-mat are old, like the same species of the same size just below the summit of Mount Marcy and other high Adirondack peaks. Both have survived extraordinary stress and added new wood very slowly to increase height and diameter. At the alpine timberline, the tundra spruce must cope with hard frosts. short growing seasons, wind, and rocky soil or no soil at all. In the bog, the same species is up against high acidity, poor oxygen supply, and nitrogen and other nutrient deficiency. The causes of their common stunting are different, the results are the same.

Timberlines, of course, are not confined to mountains. There are also timberline trees wherever a natural forest area meets some other vegetation type—prairie, desert, or tundra. An arctic timberline is found at sea-level on the delta of the mighty Mackenzie River. The forward echelon of white spruce forms a fairly definite line, but one spruce individual stands a half mile beyond any of the rest. It started growth in 1860, taking nine decades to reach a diameter of seven inches, even though no tree was nearby to shade it. The regular conical form of its crown shows that it was not trained or distorted by wind coming from a single direction during the one month of warmth sufficient for tree growth there. Yet the annual layers of wood averaged half again as wide on the sunnier south side as on the radius pointing northward; hence the pith or biological center is well north of the trunk's geometric center. The sun, never very high there, well within the Circle, is enough higher in the south than elsewhere to warm the trunk and promote more growth on that radius.

In Rocky Mountain National Park the motorist can drive for twelve miles over alpine tundra at about 12,000 feet elevation. As he approaches these heights from the east, he crosses a fascinating band of alpine timberline. On many fir trees, exposed to the prevailing westerlies, he sees a straight, erect trunk holding an arrangement of boughs reminiscent of a wind-whipped flag. The flag-form there is not caused by ice-pruning during winter storms, but solely by training of the growing parts by the summer westerlies. Any twigs that start to grow in any other direction are curved around eastward by the pressure of the air mass, and grow that way, to show the flagging when there is no wind, too.

Backpackers and mountaineers who pay some attention to the trees at and near-below timberline should be able to deduce the conditions of winter—of frost, snow, and wind separately or combined—by the tree forms and lay of the land in summer. This offers him or her something to think about besides techniques and distant scenery.

On the continental divide in central New Mexico, Bandera Crater is surrounded and overtopped by its volcanic cinder-cone. On the cooler, moister north slope of this peak overlooking the Ice Caves Trading Post, the loose ash supports tree cover up to within a few hundred feet of the rounded summit, where a single flagged pinyon pine has stood isolated for centuries at the topmost point. The highest group of trees, bordering the barren ash dome, are gnarled, sprawling pinyons about eight feet in height.

On first examining and photographing these buffeted pines on their highly scenic exposure, I found that nearly all their branches were dead and leafless. It looked as though they would have been completely dead in another five years or less. Their mineral ingredients had come from the gray volcanic ash; death and decay would soon return them there. Ashes to ashes . . .

That was in 1944. Yet in 1981 the same trees still had the same few, small portions with persistent green. New photos look no different from the original ones. Any attempt to estimate the time of their final demise would be futile, I decided. As long as one green leaf remains, or one cell in the wood or bark of the stem or root is metabolizing, the tree lives. Although the tree as an individual is ancient, each exact part in its surface community of living cells is very young. These trees are living long and intimately with death, and dying with life.

9

ELFIN RINGS

OUR ANCESTORS looked with awe on manifestations of Nature which they could not explain, but which were different enough to call for explanation. Imagination invested such things with mythic origins. Although we now have, at least in a general way, scientific explanations for their existence, we still use the names that resulted from ancient fancies.

Those phenomena that inspired awe because of overwhelming size as well as mysterious causation were often attributed to the Prince of Darkness. Examples are the Devil's Tower, Devil's Postpile, Devil's Kitchen, and Devil's Lane in as many of our National Parks and Monuments, the Devil's Slide in the Rockies, and any number of Devil's Backbones and Devil's Dens.

Satan is nothing if not ambitious; small, unspectacular, unthreatening objects of wonder were not attributed to him, but to pint-sized, usually beneficent or neutral beings such as elves. The various kinds of "elfin rings" we may find in meadows and lawns are proportioned to the scale of operations supervised by fairies and elves, or possibly by less cheerful spirits like trolls.

The basic principle, through which growth and death work out the ring form in plants, is illustrated simply and plainly in the laboratory. Some of the more attractive fungi that form colonies on the agar medium in a Petri dish left exposed to air eventually develop visible surface-growths, flat but otherwise doughnut-shaped. Some have several tightly-adhering rings of contrasting colors or tones like Saturnian rings. Growth began with a central spore which fell from the air onto the sterile nutrient agar. As the plant grows outward on all radii of the circular mass, perhaps the food under the older central part becomes exhausted, or the metabolic waste products discourage new growth in the aging central area of mold. Active growth becomes confined to the outer rings, while the original inner fungus dies away and may disappear.

The outdoor type of elfin ring seen most often, and common enough so that probably any persistent searcher of lawns should eventually spot one, is caused by several species of fairy-ring fungus. Often it is the white, bluntly-conical cap of the Inky Cap Mushroom. The underground fungal threads form the weft that is reproduced by the aboveground, spore-producing "mushroom." The white cap soon turns black and curls at the edges as it spreads and opens; it melts into a black liquid which contains the spores. The ring is marked by these mushrooms, forming a circle of sometimes forty feet in diameter or arcs of a partial circle, for only a few weeks of each year, and in lawns mowed frequently they may not be noticed. But the subterranean fungus thread-mat which produces them is there the year around. It is fixing nitrogen from the soil atmosphere whenever the soil is warm enough for its activity. Nitrogen salts stimulate the grasses to grow faster and greener in the ring-band than they do inside or outside that circle. This makes the fairy ring of grass detectable or even conspicuous during all seasons when it is not hidden by snow. The contrast is most striking when the aboveground grass is dead and sere elsewhere, but the grass of the ring, where the helpful soil fungus has not yet died out, is still green and growing. I have found conspicuous examples of such grass rings, with or without the mushrooms, on college campuses both in humid Indiana and dry southern California.

It is doubtful that plant physiologists or fungus experts have done much research on this non-economic situation, which we expect to be of greater interest to those elves small enough to sit on a toadstool.

All ranchers within the widespread range of the grass called Ring-Muhly know this *Muhlenbergia* species of dry rangelands. This is unquestionably the most common and familiar kind of plant-ring found in North America. Is it because of soil fungi or simply from using up the nutrients or soil-moisture that the Ring-Muhly dies out in the central part of the doughnut, which in my experience may reach a diameter of five or six feet?

One special, unusual habitat-type is the limy (calcareous) prairie. The Merry Lea Environmental Center in Noble County, Indiana, includes such a prairie just inland from Bear Lake. The switchgrass there grows two feet tall, too high to appropriately call its conspicuous doughnut an elfin ring. One colony is a dozen feet across the outside, and the band of living grass is about two feet across, around the open center. Could it be that an unknown root-fungus of the grass affects the chemistry of the root habitat, by decreasing harmful alkalinity?

An appropriate memorial to the notable Wisconsin ecologist John C. Curtis is the sixty-acre man-made prairie on the Madison campus. Professor Aldo Leopold had a hand in establishing this prairie community in the early Thirties. Outward growth and inner failure progressing apace enabled a wild sunflower species to form rings far larger than the switchgrass ring at Merry Lea. The botanists learned that roots of the sunflower plants release a chemical which inhibits the growth of other plants, including prairie grasses. This phenomenon, called allelopathy, is frequent in many species of grassland vegetation, affecting competition and plant succession, but seldom results in conspicuous rings as in the sunflower colony. This wild sunflower can grow vigorously and flower profusely only in the outer part of the doughnut, where other forbs and the grasses are most inhibited or suppressed.

I know of no reports of club-mosses, ferns, horsetails, or other lower vascular plants ever forming rings. Only once have I seen or heard of this happening in any of these groups. In driving along the Blue Ridge Parkway, where a 45-mile speed limit and prohibition of trucks makes car-window botanizing more feasible than from high-speed highways, I was surprised to see some highly developed elfin rings beside the road. On parking and examining them closely, I was more amazed to find that these rings, about seven feet in outside diameter, were composed of a club-moss (*Lycopodium*). The central opening was proportionately large, since the ring was mostly less than a foot wide.

Presumably there are other kinds of elfin rings not yet reported. Do let me know if you are lucky enough to spot one.

10

THE PIONEER IN NATIONAL PARK WILDLIFE MANAGEMENT

THE young naturalist from Berkeley was spending the summer of 1926 as assistant in a university survey of Mount McKinley's wildlife population. One day while tramping along a rocky ridge a thousand feet above timberline, he saw a sandpiper-like bird fly up from its eggs among the sparse tundra plants. From its white tail ending in a large black triangle he knew that it was a Surfbird, and not a Wandering Tattler which breeds in similar habitats. The student, George Wright, had known shorebirds from age thirteen when he backpacked alone along the coast from San Francisco to the Oregon line. When the bird returned to its eggs, George confirmed his Surfbird identification with care, for he knew he was making ornithological history. The nest and eggs of this species had never been reported!

George Wright, born in 1904, came early to an interest in

Nature. He started teaching natural history at age fourteen in a Boy Scout summer camp in California. As a student at the university at Berkeley, he majored in forestry, and minored in vertebrate zoology under noted zoologist Joseph Grinnell, who took young George with him to the Alaskan national park (now called Denali) for two and a half months.

George's parents were wealthy, and the young man decided to follow his interest in Nature and serve society in a low-paid career instead of piling up additional fortune. He joined the National Park Service in 1927 as Assistant Park Naturalist at Yosemite. Nowhere in the NPS at that time was there a program or full-time staff in wildlife science. This would come eventually as a result of Wright's efforts.

At Yosemite he recognized that there were too many deer for the good of the vegetation or themselves, and that they were too tame. Cougars, which should have been their chief predator if the ecosystem had been in proper balance, were probably absent altogether. Black bears, which were fed garbage each evening several miles below the village, had become a serious nuisance in the campground and elsewhere. Tule elk were not native to the park, but a small herd was being kept in the valley, confined within a paddock. Seeing all the ways in which the park's mammals were improperly handled was the stimulus which caused George to become, in a very few years, the leading exponent for wildlife science and the art of its management in the whole system of our national parks.

Resulting from his well-thought-out proposal, the first NPS wildlife survey program was set up in 1929, with headquarters at Berkeley. It was completely funded by him personally for the first two years, and half funded by him later. By 1934 it was almost entirely supported by public funds. George's influence expanded in 1934 when he headed a study commission for nationwide planning and recommending of many of the areas which were soon to become local, state, and national parks. He was also a member of the four-man team that surveyed the resources at St. John in the Virgin

Islands and urged that it become a national park. In mid-1935 Wright and his family moved to Washington, D.C. to live.

As an author, Wright promoted orderly development of biological research in the park system, and of wildlife management on a scientific basis. On his suggestion, the Interior Department started a now-famous series of books on *Fauna of the National Parks of the United States*, and he was the principal writer of the first two volumes. He was so far ahead of his time that the 1932 book still sounds modern, and has had a widespread import in determining policy and practice regarding the wildlife of the parklands here and abroad. He described environmental problems park by park, laid down essential principles of ecological management, and prescribed management solutions. However, the good sense and science in his writings might not have won acceptance nation-wide had it not been for George's sunny personality and persuasive eloquence in personal relations at high governmental levels. Biologist Lowell Sumner in 1967 recalled young Wright in these terms:

> The most effective of all his attainments and characteristics was his warm, relaxed, unselfconsciously friendly personality. But no matter how many reminiscences might be recorded concerning George Wright's disarming diplomacy, in retrospect it still seems almost unbelievable that such a young newcomer was able, in so short a period of time, to introduce a set of new management concepts into an old-line federal organization, and recruit from all over the country a team of park-oriented biologists . . . to help carry out the new ideas. To succeed, such an innovator would need an extraordinary talent for persuasiveness. . . . In addition, he had rare good luck as well as judgment in timing his efforts to take advantage of developing national resource programs.

George Wright both created and rode the crest of the first wave of attention to the ecological functioning of resources of land and life in our great parklands. As he wrote in 1932, "The conclusion is undeniable that failure to maintain the natural status of national parks fauna in spite of the presence of large numbers of visitors would also be a failure of the whole national park idea."

Tragically, he never reached his thirty-third birthday, but was killed when an oncoming car blew its tire and crashed into the one in which Wright and Roger Toll, Superintendent of Yellowstone Park, were passengers, killing them both. That was in 1936, otherwise a very good year for the parks. The recurring cycle of alternating good and poor ecological management of the parks was not to reach a comparable crest until the late Sixties. During the low period, many able scientists and administrators had quit in helpless frustration. Natural history specimens which had been laboriously assembled during Wright's ascendancy into growing study collections in the park museums, as Wright had urged, were even discarded in at least one major park.

Today the George Wright Society is active nationally. Its mission is to promote scientific research, the synthesis of information, and the useful dissemination of results to management, policy-makers, and the public in whose hands the ultimate fate of parks will rest. This organization looks at Nature in the parks from the viewpoint of modern ecosystem ecology, which was foreshadowed in 1932 by Wright and his colleagues when they wrote, "The realization is coming that our greatest natural heritage, rather than just scenic features, is Nature itself, with all its complexity and abundance of life."

Long ago a Roman philosopher, Emperor Marcus Aurelius, expressed what we now feel about the brevity of a life such as George Wright's.

> To look upon the world for a longer or briefer period makes no difference. What then is there to fear if you are sent away by the same Nature that brought you, as if the magistrate who had chosen an

actor were to dismiss him? "But I have not played the five acts, but only three." "You have played well, but in your life at any rate the three acts are the whole play." For he sets the limit who was at one time the cause of your creation, and is now the cause of your dissolution. You have no responsibility for either. So depart graciously, for he who dismisses you is also gracious.

11

WILD ANIMALS IN TAME LANDSCAPES

THIS spring a pair of Pileated Woodpeckers is nesting in a dead palm trunk in the median strip of a busy street between ranks of luxury condominiums on the Florida coast. In the business district of a more congested Florida city, a strong tapping attracted my eye to a male Pileated feeding on a dead limb of a street tree. Not long ago, perhaps a score of years, this species was seen, when it was seen at all, only in actual or almost-wilderness.

When I learned to know the Yellow-billed Cuckoo, and for many years afterward, it was a heard-but-seldom-seen species of deep broadleaf forests. But during the past two springs and early summers, these birds have often visited our yard. The latter was a treeless soy-bean field only twenty-six years ago. The secretive cuckoo can find little concealment among the small, scattered trees in our neighborhood; most of them are young pines.

As development encroaches on the Florida alligator's habitat, the alligator seems to be encroaching on man's. Sinister and tragic accounts of wild coyotes invading closely built-up sections are coming out of Los Angeles.

Bird species differ greatly in their tolerance of, or sometimes preference for, man-made habitats. The Pileated is far more adaptable than was the other giant American woodpecker, the now extinct Ivory-bill. The Red-bellied Woodpecker does very well in Florida residential developments, whereas the Red-cockaded Woodpecker has been severely hit by the cutting of slash pines and palmettos.

Clearing of the native scrub-oak cover changed the status of the Florida or Scrub Jay from common to rare, but the Blue Jay thrives in the residential areas which replaced the scrub.

A pair of ospreys is raising three chicks in a nest thirty-three feet from the fire-house in the business district on Sanibel Island. The birds appropriated a pole, and the siren horns surmounting it, as their nesting site.

Second only to birds, the giant moths are the most attractive animals of land and air. Old entomology books describe the Luna, Cecropia, and Polyphemus as "very common," and I remember them so. Between habitat loss and pesticides, these insects have dwindled drastically. A friend who teaches high school biology assigned his freshmen to turn in insect collections upon the opening of school each fall from 1948 through 1978. Fewer and fewer of the great moths were found by his students throughout this period. Lovely moths seem to be dropping out of public consciousness even more rapidly. Of the 577 pages of a popular new field guide to Nature, only two pages are devoted to moths!

Some, perhaps in time many or all, of the intolerant species will become extinct from the growth and spread of human population. It is far better when they adapt than it is for them to be exterminated. On the other hand, artificial habitats devalue our experiences with wildlife, one asset enhancing the quality of our lives. My close approach to wild Ravens in the town dump at Yellowknife, Northwest Territories, compared poorly in emotional impact with the sight of a distant Raven punctuating the sky over the Rockies. Seeing a captive lion is not the same as encountering the "king of beasts" where he belongs and we do not. A branch of science termed "urban ecology" is being developed; is this not an ecology of less interesting or exciting interrelationships? Evidently it will be *the* ecology of the future! A principal value of scenic parks and wilderness preserves is the opportunity to see wildlife living naturally. When it lives otherwise, is it really "wildlife?"

Many outdoors people assess the rewards of their Nature observations in proportion to the effort expended in making them. A zoo stands at the low end of this continuum; a wilderness in the proper sense of this much-abused word occupies the high end. A real wilderness has the large grazing and browsing animals *and their natural predators.* Deer occasionally cross my suburban lot within several feet of the house, but even the one place in Indiana officially designated as wilderness supports no cougars, bears, or wolves.

Consider the cougar. It is not that their absolute numbers are increasing, more likely the reverse. But our continuing development of their former habitats tends to concentrate the lions into fewer and smaller areas. This is worse than inconvenient to the animals, because their life-style is a wide ranging one, and its restriction brings them increasingly into confrontation with their only serious predator, man. Familiarity brings one-way contempt. And man will lose his unique respect for cougars as they become known chiefly as automobile "salesmen."

Unlike the wary cougar I barely saw at Mount Rainier in the Thirties, and only as a blurred, buffy streak vanishing among the Douglas fir trunks, the modern ones are losing their fear of man. The bears are doing likewise, and this makes the animals more dangerous than when they were numerous, sometimes heard, but seldom seen. The first serious attack on people by grizzlies in Glacier National Park that I have direct knowledge of was in 1938, when two young men were attacked on the trail and one's arm so badly mangled that it had to be amputated. He had tried to protect himself by thrusting the arm down the grizzly's throat.

In the spring of 1981 we had the opportunity to visit with old Cornell friends, the Kosters. An extra bonus was hearing of his amazing experience with a wild cougar. Dr. William J. Koster is a retired professor of zoology at the University of New Mexico; he is a highly experienced field biologist and distinctly not one to play fast and loose with facts about animals or anything else.

In March of that year he had his large dog out for a run near the head of a canyon in the Sandia Mountains, a couple of miles east of the city limits of Albuquerque. From behind a great rock near the trail came a sudden, piteous yelping, and when Bill rounded the corner he saw a full-sized mountain lion crouched on top of the profusely bleeding Labrador.

Though Koster was aware that a cougar ranging this close to a city would be familiar with and more contemptuous of man than a strictly wilderness cat, he was determined to rescue his pet if at all possible. He approached the fateful tableau slowly but directly. The predator's hoped-for fear of man did not appear to be in working order. Bill then crouched down "for a spring" in the same way as the cougar, slowly working his way closer with continuous eye contact. Finally the animal succumbed in this clash of wills, leaped to one side, and disappeared in the woods. Bill carried the limp dog to his car and rushed it to the nearest veterinary office. The doctor finally saved its life, but averred that it would have died if bleeding had continued for another fifteen seconds! We saw the grievous scars on the dog's head, neck, and body.

On reporting this extraordinary incident to an official of the federal wildlife agency, Bill agreed to take him to the site the next day for a thorough investigation. Tracks in the snow fully substantiated his account of events. The other biologist measured the distances involved. Man and cat had been only seventeen feet apart when the latter decided that he was less hungry for dog than he was concerned about the unfamiliar creature that had a scent like a human but appeared quite willing to meet in claw-to-claw combat.

12

LINN RUN AND LITTLE PINE CREEK

IN the Allegheny Mountains, a cold trout-stream hurries down from the heights of the Laurel Ridge. In 1920, the Pennsylvania forestry bureau first offered the leasing privilege there to private families. The first to sign up was my father. He leased for twenty years a half-acre of white rhododendron, hemlock, and yellow birch bordering Linn Run.

That August, a horse and buggy rented in Ligonier carried the family of six with camping gear along an old logging trail that no vehicle had negotiated in years. The old timber railroad, from which the rails had been removed but the ties left, would have been even worse, and the antique wagon trail did cross our new land. Mudholes and big rocks made it nearly impassable, but the most difficult feat was getting down to Linn Run at the ford, blundering through the boulders and torrent there, and up the rocky slope beyond. The poor horse lost his footing time and again, the rig would lurch wildly, and my three terrified little sisters augmented the excitement. Fortunately, Dad was a skilled hand with horses.

Before our second summer there, the state had pulled up the chestnut ties and made the old railroad into a passable dirt road. It was used for delivery of our order of rough lumber for Dad and me to build a comfortable cottage on the high terrace thirty feet from the stream. Linn Run's rushing waters were to lull us to sleep on most August nights for twenty years. Mother named the place Camp Glen Lynn. For all the time there, we healthfully drank the waters of the stream.

Dad, a Methodist minister, had a strong emotional attachment to Nature; Mother had a more scientific interest in outdoor things. Because the appointments policy of the Pittsburgh Conference was to move ministers at intervals not exceeding five years, we lived in many parsonages. Camp Glen Lynn became our real family home. This was the place where I first became apprenticed to Nature. I roamed the forest trails, talked with the old-timers, fished, studied trees and birds, and scourged the rattlesnake and copperhead population.

One afternoon a solitary fly-fisherman stopped at our cabin to borrow a yardstick. He particularly asked Dad to note that his largest brook trout was twenty-three and a half inches long. A week later he showed up again, without fishing tackle, having brought another fisherman eighty miles for but one purpose. After confirming the fact that Dad was a preacher and not a fisherman, and the fact that he had watched the big trout being measured, he asked the crucial question, "How long was that fish?" Perhaps the friend, noting the mere fifteen-foot width of Linn Run, remained skeptical of Dad's twenty-three and a half inch answer.

* * *

The author of the *Flora of Indiana*, Charles C. Deam, considered the lower valley of Little Pine Creek as the best place in the state for wildflowers. When he told me this, he was not aware that I owned week-end recreational property along the stream there. We used it in raising children as my parents had used Camp Glen Lynn.

In 1891, the hardscrabble farmer there had cut down many white pines in the northwest cove. He snaked the logs across the thirty-foot creek, squared them with his broad-axe, and built a two-story four-room house on the high terrace. It was a lovely wooded valley, but the land proved an "uneconomic unit" for farming, a fact stated more simply by the old woman who sold it to us in 1948. She was of pioneer stock, and could sign the papers only with her "X." With two other faculty families, we bought her eighty acres of woods, over-grazed pasture, and flood plain cornfield. I got less than a third of the land, but all of the culture because we had the youngest children. In the former open acreage, the three families planted small Scotch pines for marketing Christmas tree crops. This greatly amused a ninety-year old neighbor (also unable to read or write), who said his father had settled in this valley and had cut down all the trees he could, and now we came in and planted them back!

The white pine seedlings that our children planted on the hillside behind the cabin are now fourteen inches in diameter. Their soft foliage catches the breeze and the mat of dead needles prevents soil erosion. Our girl had a rope swing in the venerable cottonwood tree that shaded the cabin. From her high tree-house in a tree near the creek, she seemed able to hear the pipes of Pan. The boy had his den on the hillside under the exposed roots of a spreading sycamore.

They both learned to swim in the deep hole at the bend of the creek, off the gravel bar we used for picnics and sunning. Little Pine is a restless stream. The kids would haul out for a

66

breather on the two-ton rock which in 1948 was barely exposed in the cut bank, but which seemed gradually to creep across the stream year after year until it finally disappeared under the flood plain on the opposite side. In winter the frozen pools furnished slick fun.

Deam was right about the wildflowers. For example, one cluster of the extremely rare, small variety of yellow *Cypripedium* measured four feet in diameter, and displayed about forty slipper flowers each spring. On a shady knoll the blue and white birdsfoot violets spread their artistically designed leaves at the edge of the shadow cast by a stout, low-branched white oak. The spring woodland beckoned us to enjoy its varied and profuse display of flowers. In the evening dusk, a pair of whip-poor-wills would call back and forth in the deeper shadows somewhere.

In our time there, the stream's monarch was the big red-horse sucker in the spawning ground. In more remote times, the mammoth had owned this region, and we found evidence of this after a flood which washed a huge, corrugated molar tooth into the shallows.

In the narrow portion of the valley just upstream from the eighty acres, we found high sandstone bluffs. Erosion had undercut them at many points to form shallow, maple-shaded caverns. Waterfalls and seeps along these cliffs were transformed in winter into fairylands of fantasy. In one such recess after the spring thaw, one finds each May 10 the black spore-bearing spheres of the liverwort *Pellia*, borne on white, light-sensitive stalks that here lie flat on the leafy part because the light comes into the cavern sidewise.

The children, the only valuable product of this farm, had the run of the entire eighty. The sense of place, so necessary for growing humans, is still stronger in them for Pine Valley than for their home in town. The place means as much to them in maturity as the laurel-shaded spot along Linn Run means to my three sisters and me of the previous generation.

13

"LET NATURE BE YOUR TEACHER"

WORDSWORTH did not advocate letting Nature be your *only* teacher. That came close to happening, however, to some children who grew up to sit among the immortals beside Nature's throne.

Young Jean Audubon lived near Nantes, France, from age five to eighteen without receiving much formal education. He was a "natural child" in more than one way, happily roaming and hunting from an early age. He drew the common birds without realizing how original that effort was, especially when he depicted them with the associated plants. Jean was given lessons in music, dancing, fencing, and quickly learned to play the flute, violin, and flageolet. He studied drawing very briefly in Paris.

His father Captain Audubon worried about the boy's future, and decided that it would be brighter in America. Thus, at eighteen the lad came to live in a big stone house on a hill overlooking the Perkiomen River near Valley Forge. Although his father wished him to learn to manage the estate, he spent most of his time in hunting, fishing, speed-skating, taxidermy, painting, music, and dancing. He invented a way of using stiff wires to pose birds for his paintings. When he met the wealthy, sixteen-year-old neighbor Lucy Bakewell (later Audubon), he added portraiture to his artistic interests. His first two hundred bird paintings were destroyed in the box where he stored them. Probably Art owes a substantial debt to the Norway rats which shredded the paintings for nesting material.

"Nature, the kind old nurse, took the child upon her knee." This was surely true at a very early age for Geneva Stratton, the youngest of twelve children on the family farm along the Wabash River. Her fragile mother and farmer-preacher-outdoorsman father realized that their daughter was a rare sort and did not try too hard or too early to domesticate her. With her four youngest brothers she fished, hunted, swam, and learned about wild things in the meadows and woods, and made friends with the chiefs and their families in two nearby Indian reservations. Many of her early experiences were to go into twenty-one books she was to write as Gene Stratton Porter.

The girl never got around to finishing high school, and was not interested in going to college as some of her siblings did. She read very widely, and mastered the piano, organ, and violin adequately. She taught herself oil painting, watercolor painting, became a photographer of professional caliber, and used these arts to illustrate her seven straight Nature-books, her most permanent writings. The author was not the heroine of her *Girl of the Limberlost*, for that swamp of beauty and mystery, now long lost, was not part of her youth. Mrs. Porter's most autobiographic novel is *Laddie*, in which the narrator Little Sister lived the same outdoor life in which the author reveled as a child. The hero is her favorite brother, who in real life was drowned in the Wabash. I consider this novel a classic portrayal of how life was in the rural Midwest near the end of the pioneer period.

She claimed that her fiction works were books on Nature rather than novels, but literary critics, innocent of botany and zoology, were not kind in their judgments. Though her fiction is too sentimental and wholesome for modern readers, it perfectly matched the popular taste of the day and attracted fifty million readers in seven languages. At the very edge of the old swamp just south of Geneva, Indiana, she built the fourteen room "Limberlost Cabin" of cedar logs from Wisconsin, and lived there with her druggist-banker husband from 1895 to 1913. In the latter year she built, in her 150-acre Wildflower Woods along Sylvan Lake, an eighteen-room "log cabin," with a superb photographic darkroom, and hired five men to transplant into the woods the rare wildflowers being extirpated by drainage projects and land-use patterns elsewhere. Both mansions are now open to the public, maintained as state memorials.

Mrs. Porter's works, not great in the literary sense, were extremely influential in a different way, one for which she never was given due credit. Her books, along with those of Seton and Muir especially, prepared the public mind to receive from Theodore Roosevelt's "bully pulpit" the preachments which brought about the first of our two great environmental movements.

In Scotland, young John Muir vied with playmates in counting bird's nests and eggs, and in unbelievably long, swift runs through the countryside. Alone, it delighted him to watch and listen to the skylarks. "Wildness was ever sounding in our ears," he wrote in the fascinating account of his boyhood and youth. Both in the Scottish schools and at home he was taught from the rear, by stern discipline, which he wrote later was "utterly devoid of fun." But "No punishment, however sure and severe, was of any avail against the attraction of the fields and woods." From these beginnings of his lifelong wanderings onwards, Muir remained one of those select human beings unable to look upon the natural world with an even pulse.

In America, from age eleven to twenty-two in rural Wisconsin, he attended school for only two months. For his later career as literary naturalist and national park advocate, Nature taught him *what* to put into his books. The "how" of writing them was, I think, inspired largely by his having learned before age eleven, "by heart and sore flesh," to recite verbatim all of the New Testament and three-fourths of the Old. This John became the bearded prophet, crying for the wilderness, whom we must thank for the best of our present national park system. He also, as a young man, originated the concept of preserving small natural areas. Three decades after he had tried to preserve such an area by purchase, he mentioned the idea to his creation the Sierra Club, but it was an idea which, even then in 1895, would be adopted by the Nature Conservancy only a half-century later.

Another "little savage" was the boy Ernest Thompson Seton, one of ten sons of a prominent Scotch family. When he was almost six, the family left England for Canada, and lived in a pioneer cabin near Lindsay, Ontario. There Ernest spent every spare moment in the surrounding woods, passionate to know the name and nature of all the wild things he saw. The books he was able to consult were too technical for the youngster. Field guides for easy identification did not exist; he was to grow up and invent the principle of recognition marks on which they are based.

Ernest's eyesight was weak. He improved his precarious health by vigorous outdoor exercise and became a physically powerful and impressive man. He not only took up taxidermy like Theodore Roosevelt and other young naturalists of the time, but became skilled at drawing and painting birds and mammals. Even though he later attended traditional art academies in London and Paris, as both an animal artist and a naturalist he remained self-trained. That is to say, he continued as a pupil in Nature's no-room country school.

His boyhood experiences were woven into his unique books, especially *Two Little Savages* (1902) in which the main character Yan is really young Seton. Expressing his motive for authorship, the entire preface is, "Because I have known the torment of thirst I would dig a well where others may drink." Two generations of outdoor biologists drank from his books the inspiration for their subsequent careers in the study of Nature. Millions of other children still get draughts of the wild vintage through the Boy Scouts of America, which he founded in 1910 and served for five years as Chief Scout. Later he helped found Girl Scouting.

Enos A. Mills was far and away the greatest mountaineer among literary naturalists. He was more truly the father of Rocky Mountain National Park than any other individual was responsible for any other great park on this continent. Some men, like Zebulon Pike, discovered the bodies of our mountains. Mills discovered their souls.

Enos was born in 1870 near Fort Scott, Kansas. His mother filled his imagination with tales of the wonders she had seen in Colorado; the boy left home for there and made his own living from age fourteen. He was not only self-educated in general, but he also made himself a naturalist by the method advised by Agassiz—"Study Nature, not books." At sixteen, Enos homesteaded a parcel of land and solitude at the base of Long's Peak, now within the east edge of the national park. Well ahead of his time, he recorded much of what we now term the ecology of the Rockies, both plant and animal. He originated the idea of snow surveying, and worked at this for the state irrigation bureau. Like young Muir, he was a highly skilled mechanic, and at twenty-two worked as chief engineer at an Anaconda company mine.

Never carrying a gun, he would roam the mountains for weeks on end. A discerning friend wrote, "There was nothing about the man or his opinions that was standardized. He formed his judgments . . . irrespective of what the majority thought. He was intensely original and individual. Such men are extremely rare." They are also, as Mills was, usually self-employed.

Mills bought Long's Peak Inn, and after it burned he rebuilt it himself "so that it would not frighten the peaks and scenery." He made it a mecca for the vacationing naturalists, amateur and professional. There he founded what he called the profession of "nature guiding," now an important activity in national and other parks and in countless nature centers and outdoor museums. His seventeen books showed that Nature had taught him well from early youth, for Mills has not been surpassed as an original, accurate and untiring observer of wild animals and birds.

John Burroughs represented for scores of years to the public the archetype of the graybeard naturalist. He grew up, a thoughtful child, on a hill farm in the Catskills. The boy attended a typical country school, but learned little about Nature there. Between the hours in school and the farm chores, John's waking hours were devoted to fascinated explorations of the wild, especially birds and flowers. With insatiable curiosity and retentive memory, he built up a mental collection of natural lore and meditations upon which he continued to draw throughout a long writing career.

Except for a few youthful years as a federal employee in Washington, where he knew Walt Whitman well enough to write the first biography of that poet, Burroughs' writing was done in natural surroundings, often at Slabsides near his Hudson River house. But in the summers he returned to his boyhood haunts, where he sat and wrote just inside the wide-open barn door at his Woodchuck Lodge, in sight of his father's farm across the valley.

Perhaps the most useful boyhood activity, long term, had been lying hour after hour of summer days upon a flat-topped boulder, watching the changing cloud-forms and listening to the voices of life. What could have a deeper influence on an embryonic philosopher and poet of Nature than such work in the library of the living? Today, what was mortal of John Burroughs rests in the soil of home beside that rock of his boyhood that overlooks the hill pasture and the woods beyond.

It is hardly surprising that outstanding naturalists have had strong interest in Nature when very young, since children in general have not yet lost their innate curiosity, and are far better than the average adult at observing minute things. In his 1864 book *Man and Nature*, George Perkins Marsh wrote, "The power most important to cultivate, and, at the same time, the hardest to acquire, is that of seeing what is before us." I believe that the difficulty is not in acquiring this power, but in retaining it from the days of childhood. Above all, a child's vision of what is important in life has not yet been determined by the traditional viewpoints, which are later to be imposed upon it by the adult world.

14

CHILD'S PLAY

THE average age for starting adolescence in America, physiologists say, is eleven. This has not changed in three score years, but much else has, including the amount of free time children enjoy and what is done with it.

Between the two of us, we may be able to go back temporarily to the period of the wall-phone, hatpin, straight razor, feather bed, glass milk-bottle, electric car, iceman, scissors grinder, and itinerant peddler. Sending a letter cost two cents, but one could economize with a one-cent postal card instead. For decades still to come, the postman would make two deliveries daily. The minister walked all over town making regular calls on perfectly healthy parishioners, as well as those ill or troubled. The main rounds that doctors made were through the town and countryside, not the hospital. The psychiatrists were still in Vienna.

Every town had at least one baseball team consisting of grown men who played the game for fun. Traveling circuses brought excitement for the small fry. Each summer a movable cultural feast, the Redpath Chautauqua, put up a big tent and folding wooden chairs and stayed in town for a week. The annual Sunday School picnic was a big event; committed adults left for a week of camp-meeting and old-time religion once a year.

Calling movie theaters "nickelodeons" correctly indicated the price of admission for young and old. Our favorite stars were William S. Hart, Pearl White, Charlie Chaplin, Harry Carey, and Francis X. Bushman. The word "cliff-hanger" was suggested by such Saturday matinee serials as

Perils of Pauline, the Iron Claw, and the Clutching Hand. Some of them ran more than twenty weeks. The heroes were readily distinguishable from the villains. At too rare intervals, a traveling show with a couple of live Indians would play at the nickelodeon. Our side had just won, we thought, the first and last world war.

A young boy wore knee breeches with a folding knife in a pocket, and long black stockings with garters of white elastic. The donning of one's first pair of long pants was a thrilling rite of passage. If bicycles are regarded as primarily for transport, the only popular mechanical toys were Lionel trains, Erector sets, and perhaps Tinker Toys. Every boy I knew made a sidewalk scooter by taking apart one old roller skate, affixing the front and back pairs of wheels near the ends of a footboard, which was a convenient length of two-by-four. To its front end was fastened a vertical two-by-four, topped with a small cross-piece for the handles. Powered by the left foot, this conveyance made a most satisfactory noise on concrete sidewalks.

Even in respectable neighborhoods there were frequent recreational fights among small boys. Most parents seemed to consider this a normal developmental stage, but tended to frown on it at the bloody nose and knocked-out-teeth level of intensity. Legal standards have evolved since then, and in 1982 a six-year-old girl in Florida struck a playmate, was apprehended by police, and barely escaped being tried as an adult for assault.

You could not become a Boy Scout, Girl Scout, Campfire Girl, Lone Scout, or Woodcraft Indian until you were twelve, and no longer a child. The Young Men's Christian Association was open to young girls only once a week, for swimming and gymnasium. Unrestricted open country with its meadows, woods and streams was plentiful. Small-town and rural lads spent much time with their pals in natural swimming holes at the bends of creeks, overhung by a single long rope-swing ending in a knot, and without an old tire either on the rope or in the pool. Boys often went fishing or hunting alone, or trapped fur-bearers for pin money and adventure. After graduating from hollow bean-shooters, then slingshots of strong rubber bands on a forked stick, and a Daisy air rifle, one might aspire to a .22 rifle. In winter, we rode our Flexies at breath-taking speed down slopes where all Hupmobiles, Haines, Dodge Brothers, Reos, and Pierce Arrows were temporarily excluded from the intersections over long stretches. Sledders and ice-skaters congregated at bonfires in the evenings to warm the body and spirit.

The basic social institution affecting children was not the school, or even the church, but the family. The young were encouraged and eased gently into adulthood, not pressured into it. The time for dating was not late at night, but late in youth. It is not really a contradiction to state that children were bound closely to parents morally and spiritually but were generally allowed much freedom from early in life.

Lacking radio, television, Little League, Cub Scouts, Brownies, star war-games, and organized football teams in grade school, and with relatively few other contributions except books by extra-family adults, children were able to entertain themselves. The boys, especially, were free to do so because mothers lacked packaged and pre-cooked foods and labor-saving devices, and had more children and little need to worry about their safety away from home.

Most games and pastimes were independent of adults, were not pre-packaged or purchased, and were usually sex-segregated. Boys were worried about being called "sissy;" girls "tom-boy." Strange, primitive half-games, more aggression-dominance rituals, pleased the boys, but girls would not think of engaging in such fighting-once-removed, for they understood that they were constituted of "sugar and spice, and everything nice." Mothers tried to teach girls to be lady-like, with reasonable success; the term lady was not considered applicable to cleaning-women, hired girls, or loose women. Girls learned at home the domestic skills and social graces they were expected to need as adults. Little girls adored their grade-school and Sunday-school teachers, and enjoyed helping mother with the younger children. Lest anyone might look back upon those times with unalloyed nostalgia, she should first realize that this general approach to child-rearing would be deplored by the liberated modern.

Marbles, mumble-de-peg, plain and fancy tricks and battles with spinning wooden tops, duck-on-a-rock, kick the can, and generally I Spy and kite-flying were for young boys. Sidewalk roller skating most of the year and ice-skating in winter were popular with both sexes. Girls played with dolls and doll-houses, made mud pies, sewed, played jacks, Hop Scotch, London Bridge, Up-a-Step, and skipped rope.

Many of the girls' routines, like the dances of Maoris and other primitives, were accompanied by repetitive chanting, chatter, and rigamarole, learned word-for-word from other girls. The minimal degree of organization needed for such activities was provided by the kids themselves. Incidentally, the use of "kid" for other than a young goat was considered mildly salacious by the genteel.

How old must a reader be to remember the expert multiple rope-skipping with its ancient, complex chants, or the sight of a young girl happily amusing herself all of a summer afternoon with a rubber ball and jacks and her sing-song accompaniment? I expect only those in my own generation to realize that a Hop-Scotch court chalked on the sidewalk is an atavistic relic of a distinct, antiquated child-culture, as interesting and significant as the human cultures which anthropologists go to remote regions to study. Perpetuated for centuries by children under twelve, it is completely disregarded in a scholarly recent book on small town America and its history. Children, even more than women, have been invisible to historians.

While this child-culture dwindled away, the modern teenage culture, also distinct from that of adults, proliferated amazingly. The least commercialized and mechanized portion of teen culture is the game Dungeons and Dragons, which fascinates many teen intellectuals whereas it mystifies adults. But in most aspects, as in electronic games, record albums, and drugs, teen culture is now dependent upon and exploited by adult business enterprise. The old child culture was largely independent of that.

I hope that kids really used to have as much fun as I remember.

15

PRESIDENTIAL FAREWELL TO PASSENGER PIGEONS

THE HISTORIC, weather-beaten cottage gradually revealed itself through the leafless trees as my walk down the lane neared an end. My long search for Pine Knot, the old presidential hideaway in western Virginia, was over.

It was early 1976. The bare oak trees stood becalmed in thin April sunshine, gathering from it the energy needed for their spring explosion. The cottage was still there, and so was the solitude beloved by Theodore and Edith Roosevelt. How much does this modest house, a former sharecropper's cabin, remember of its distinguished owners? It seemed unchanged since the day of TR's 1906 photograph, except that the cottontail rabbits he had bagged for the evening meal were not now hanging on the wall in the shade of a chimney. One felt that at any moment the brooding stillness might be broken by the creaking of saddle-leather or by a rustling of fallen leaves from footfalls of a stocky figure strolling among the trees.

The President wrote his son Kermit in early June of 1905: "Mother and I have just come from a lovely trip to Pine Knot. It is really a perfectly delightful little place. . . . Mother is a great deal more pleased with it than any child with any toy I ever saw." Edith had just bought the cabin and fifteen surrounding acres of woods, and TR hired Dick McDaniel to build at each end a chimney and fireplace of native stone. Later, another seventy-five wooded acres were added. The President named the place Pine Knot because of the six knotty-trunks of pine trees that support the porch roof. The couple usually took breakfast on the porch to hear the morning bird chorus, doubtless including the three-note song of the Cardinal: "Theodore! Theodore!" Although Roosevelt died in 1919, Edith and the family kept the property until 1941.

Although TR is usually thought of today as more conservationist than naturalist, he was a field biologist of professional caliber. He was also a part-time professional literary-naturalist, since many of his thirty-eight books are on his observations and enjoyment of Nature. He had majored in biology at Harvard, fully intending to make science his life work, but changed his career plans because biology was dominated by microscopy and absorption in minutiae.

Roosevelt's reputation as a man of action is a half-truth; he was equally a man of thought, a scholarly man who knew better than to talk like one on either the wilderness trail or the campaign trail. His only weakness as an intellectual was that he had no weak opinions. The three intellectuals who have occupied the White House were Jefferson, the first Roosevelt, and Wilson. TR had more of warmth, humor, and the common touch than the other two combined. At Pine Knot and elsewhere he found in Nature the respite from official cares that Lincoln had found in humor.

The greatest American presidents were those who saw their responsibilities to the future and acted on them. TR was one of only two presidents awarded the Nobel Peace Prize, which was not given because of the most permanent contribution he made to the world—his practice of an enlightened ethic where it is most difficult and, in the long term, most important to do so—toward the rights and needs of future generations. The worldwide environmental movement he inaugurated and the living wildlands he set aside from ordinary exploitation commemorate Theodore Roosevelt more suitably then his visage on Mount Rushmore or even his statue in the 88-acre nature preserve on Roosevelt Island opposite the Watergate complex.

Roosevelt's most memorable wildlife experience took place at Pine Knot. It was one no longer possible for anyone, anywhere. He sighted and observed for some time a flock of passenger pigeons, a bird species that most ornithologists believed was then already extinct. TR first reported the sighting, of the last wild flock of what was once the most abundant bird in the world, to the U.S. Biological Survey and to his friend John Burroughs who was keeping track of wild pigeon records and reports. Five months later, TR included the sighting in his lead article in Scribners Magazine:

On May 18, 1907, I saw a small party of . . . passenger pigeons, birds I had not seen for a quarter of a century and never expected to see again. I saw them two or three times flying hither and thither with great rapidity, and once they perched in a tall dead pine on the edge of an old field. They were unmistakable, yet the sight was so unexpected that I almost doubted my eyes, and welcomed a bit of corroborative evidence coming from Dick McDaniel, . . . a frequent companion of mine in rambles around the country . . . an unusually close and accurate observer of birds and of wild things generally.

One of the attractions that Edith and her husband held

out to John Burroughs in inviting him to Pine Knot for four days was the possibility that the pigeons would still be around. Oom John, as TR always addressed him, replied accepting for the visit, but expressed skepticism that anyone could see pigeons at that late date. On their bird walks around Pine Knot, the two naturalists listed seventy-five kinds of birds; each taught the other two species new to him. After the President's death, Burroughs wrote an account of this visit, stating that TR had known the warblers in the trees overhead during that spring migration as well as he did himself. Roosevelt was particularly expert from boyhood on bird songs and calls.

During this visit by John O'Birds, the friends together interviewed McDaniel about all aspects of his sighting of forty-five passenger pigeons six days before TR's experience. His observations agreed with Roosevelt's in every particular except for the larger number in the flock. Dick was familiar with passenger pigeons from his youth, and these were the first he had seen in decades. Burroughs wrote at the time that, despite initial skepticism, he was now convinced that both men had seen passenger pigeons. Ornithologists at the American Museum of Natural History also accepted TR's record, clinched for them by Roosevelt's having seen mourning doves simultaneously for comparison.

The last specimen authenticated as to date of collection was a single bird shot in August, 1906, in Fairfield County, Connecticut. A small flock captured in 1878 had been established in the Cincinnati Zoo and eventually produced Martha, the last individual of her species. This living symbol of a lost wild America died at age twenty-nine in 1914. Her passing and that of a remarkable bird species occurred fifty-seven years after the Ohio legislature had declared, "The passenger pigeon needs no protection. Wonderfully prolific . . ."

Roosevelt's dozen birds, so far as science and history can determine, were the last free passenger pigeons. TR could have rushed back to Pine Knot for his shotgun and collected a specimen for absolute confirmation, but he was quite certain of his identification and wrote, "Nothing could have persuaded me to shoot them."

Having other things on his mind, the President probably never realized that he was the last trained, qualified naturalist ever to see wild passenger pigeons. Whether he was also the last human being to see them will never be known. I should like to think that he was, and he may very well have been. His distaste for going back for his gun to clinch his observation beyond any conceivable question should not deprive this life-long naturalist of the most dramatic bird record of the twentieth century.

16

THE FOREST PRIMEVAL AND ITS PEOPLE

THE United States Department of Justice enlisted our help in reconstructing the northern third of Indiana as it had been in the first quarter of the previous century, though strictly on paper. Both sides in a $50. million Indian-claims case needed solid data on the early status of that area in terms of forests and prairie, topography, soils, and drainage. This was my opportunity to spend a year in the wilderness of the

Northwest Territories during the days of Tecumseh and Little Turtle.

The Miami and Potawatomi tribes hoped to establish as valid their claim before the Indian Claims Commission, which, though including no Native Americans, usually rules in favor of the claimants.

Ecologists probe the past by the following methods, in rough order of increasing depth of penetration backward: permanent quadrat plots, old photographs, timberline studies, fire scars on trees, land surveyor's records, historical writings, fluctuations of extant glaciers, tree-ring analysis, pollen analysis in bogs and lake-bottoms, and radiocarbon dating. For environmental studies of times before about 50,000 years ago, more distinctively geological methods are needed. The most appropriate technique for my study was detailed analysis of the explicit and voluminous records of the original land survey of the state, 1795-1847. The chairman of the federal group that originated and instituted the Township-Range method of survey was that versatile Virginian, Thomas Jefferson.

The field leaders were both trained surveyors and skilled woodsmen who lived off the land during their rectilinear travels. Each "town" of thirty-six square miles (sections) was platted to show section and quarter section lines, streams, lakes, ponds, swamps, marshes, and bogs. Also recorded were Indian villages, land grants, white settlements and farms if any, prairies, salt licks, and other features worth noting.

For each township a form was provided for writing up running descriptions of the physiography, drainage conditions, soil quality, timber species and other vegetational notes, and a variety of other natural things. Another form was for the systematic recording of witness (or "bearing" trees, for compass-bearing) and this was the most useful of the old records for our work. It was intended to make possible the relocation of section and quarter-section corners. Thus, for each half-mile north-south and east-west in a forest, at least two and often four trees were located and described for the permanent record.

By applying to these data the methods by which modern plant ecologists analyze presently existing stands of timber, I was able to reconstruct the forest as it was originally, in about the same way ecologists now report on an extant area of forest. Then on the very detailed modern soil maps of counties, I could spot the precise soil type (of the 300+ in this state) where each tree had been growing. Thus, I learned how well or poorly each tree species was adapted to each soil type, or how it responds to chemical and physical factors separated out in statistical analyses by computer. Mature trees are not studied in laboratories and greenhouses, since they are too large and take scores of years to grow, but by this new approach I used "experimental material" that had grown under conditions of unrivalled naturalness. The whole of forested Indiana was used for this part of the study, and we learned the relative influence of each of the many soil and drainage factors that influence tree growth and success.

Not all of our Midwest had been "owned" by Indians, for early Indians generally agreed with Tecumseh that the sun was their father and the Earth was their mother, and they did not care to sell their mother. The early US government had gone through the motions of purchase, usually so as to satisfy the legalisms of the time. However, the (white) attorneys alleged on behalf of the tribes that purchase treaties undervalued the unimproved land, and that the nation had let its installment payments lapse but gave the original occupants no opportunity to repossess the property. Much of Indiana, though, had been used as a common hunting ground by various wandering tribes at one time or another. In our case, a final consolidation of fifteen earlier ones, the settlement went against the Indians because the Commission found that they had not proved "aboriginal title." The attorneys for the tribes would have been paid $5. million had they won, but got nothing for years of work. Still, Indian claims cases were said at the time to provide the most profitable form of law practice.

The ghost forest I studied contained many huge trees, but much of it was not dense woods, the "dark and bloody ground" of popular tradition. The term "virgin timber" had become rather meaningless after millennia of Indian use. These people moved their villages and maize fields frequently, and often burned brushlands and prairies to keep the cover open for deer.

The most striking change in the last century and a half, aside from the loss of forests to the white man's cultivation, was conversion of the surface from wet to dry. The Potawatomi Indians had lived on remote islands in the productive Eden of marshes and swamps. In times of flooding, white voyageurs could paddle their big freight canoes across the portages from the Lake Michigan to the Ohio or Lake Erie drainages, without unloading. The original surveyors mapped a 28,000-acre lake (Beaver Lake) where the modern motorist on US 41 from Chicago to Terre Haute crosses the middle of it and sees no water. Waterfowl were so abundant in the wetlands south of Lake Michigan that many early sportsmen from Europe and our eastern states came there for the best duck and goose hunting anywhere.

Vast areas of natural wetlands were eliminated by agricultural drainage of the Midwest. For instance, we determined that 50.3 per cent of Indiana north of the Wabash had been ponded, in presettlement times, for at least six months during a year of normal precipitation. In one county that was 69 per cent wetland, the pioneers called the tall-grass prairie "the lost lands," never expecting it could be farmed. Today, these are the richest agricultural lands in the state, their black soils unsurpassed in the world for productivity. Throughout the survey reports on these lands, the only time the deputy surveyors let emotion creep into their records was in describing the indescribable mires they had to traverse. From 1885 on, the tiling and ditching of land, and dredging and straightening of streams, has made a drastic but little-appreciated change from earlier conditions. Malaria was once a serious plague to settlers in this relatively northern region.

The Passenger Pigeon, once the most abundant North American bird, went with the undisturbed ecosystem. It was the drastic reduction of hardwood forests with their acorns, beech nuts, and other wildlife "mast," as well as the hounding by market hunters and farmers, that caused its extermination. Breeding them in zoos, the method now being proposed for endangered mammals and birds, proved unsuccessful. Such last-resort programs are acts of desperation, for a drastic element in extermination, the loss of most genetic variations in the population that insures the potential of a species, has already occurred. There is no real substitute for preservation of natural habitats.

Although prairie soils are superior to forest soils for agriculture, many pioneers were deeply suspicious of a soil that did not support forest. While trees had many uses, Midwestern forests offered an embarrassment of riches. Often magnificent logs, such as are no longer seen, were rolled into piles or dumped into ravines and burned, with the help of neighbors during a "bee." Crops were commonly grown among the long-lasting stumps. On one homestead a non-conformist farmer from New York used the eastern method, clearing the land completely, and enjoyed half again as large a crop as his neighbors who merely girdled the trees.

Windfall was important in producing openings and "edges" favorable to wildlife. The deputy (field) surveyors clearly indicated on their plats the boundaries of devastated areas in forests. They mapped ninety-nine such tornado tracks in Indiana. Forty-four of these represented large tornadoes leaving swaths more than a quarter-mile wide. It is certain that many tracks went unrecorded, for early instructions did not call for noting them, and in any case the surveyors traversed only the exterior lines of the (square mile) sections.

Indian villages marked on the plat show a distinct relation to previous tornadoes. Besides liking to be near streams for transport, Indians preferred the proximity of an old tornado track where a practically unlimited supply of dry, dead fuel was available. The present village of Windfall, Indiana, has grown from a few buildings between two areas of down timber on Wildcat Creek. About 1830 a tornado occurred with exactly the same location and course as the fateful twister of Palm Sunday 1965 which devastated Russiaville and killed 160 people.

In 1805 the surveyors platted and described the quarter-section where Thomas Lincoln was soon to settle his family. There has been so much loose writing about the boyhood of Abraham Lincoln that the facts supplied in the survey records are revealing.

Since the clerk in Washington who transcribed the deputy surveyor's field notes happened to write the description of the south boundary into the wrong place on the official form, I looked up the actual field-book which was carried in 1805 to the 160 acres where young Lincoln's bone, sinew, and mind were to be molded by the natural and human environment.

The first survey there had recorded witness trees in these species percentages, by the common names we still use: black oak 29 per cent, white oak 18, hickory 18, dogwood 14, gum 8, elm 4, cherry 3, maple 2, and black walnut 1 per cent. Minor trees were "plumb," red oak, persimmon, sassafras, yellow poplar, and crab apple. It was clearly an oak-hickory type forest, not the beech-maple or mixedwoods types also found in the Midwest.

The Lincoln cabin was on a knoll, not, as placed by some accounts, "on the banks of Little Pigeon Creek," since only an eight-foot wide tributary of that stream was within their land. The southern boundary of their land was "Level and rich, Jack Ok (sic), Black Oak, Hickory, etc." The west boundary was termed "Flat brushy briery oak-timbered soil." The ranking of black oak first in individual numbers shows that the land was too well drained to be good for farming. Sugar maple dominance would have indicated good, moist, calcium-rich soil, but this species was rare. The high ranking of dogwood, and the brieriness, clearly show that the timber was not dense. The oak-hickory type indicates land generally inferior for farming to that of the beech-maple type. There in Carter Township, young Abraham from age 7 to 21 became intimately acquainted with trees, their species properties and uses. Edwin Markham put it differently:

> *"His words were oaks in acorns; and his thoughts*
> *Were roots that firmly gripped the granite truth."*

After nearly two years residence there, Nancy Hanks Lincoln died from milk-sickness, as had several near neighbors. We now know that this "disease" was caused by the poison trematol from the wild herb white snakeroot (*Eupatorium rugosum*) eaten by cattle. The stream that traversed the family acreage provided an ideal flood plain habitat, from which the plant invaded man-made clearings and was eaten by cattle. The "milk-sick" was a serious scourge while forests were being cleared wholesale in southern Indiana and the plant was a likely item of cattle food.

Dennis Hanks lost both his foster parents from this, then mysterious, ailment. He proposed and accompanied the Lincoln family trek to Illinois, explaining in a letter, "Reson is this we war perplext by a disease cald Milk Sick . . . I was determed to leve and hunt a country where the milk was not . . ." Thus, a poisonous herb with unfortunate ecological relationships not only killed Abraham's mother but also unsettled his life at the crucial age of manhood. If his family had stayed on the hard-scrabble farm in sparsely-settled, culturally deprived Spencer County, Abe *might* still have made the break from his parents, educated himself, and found his way into politics. But it certainly seems much less likely.

17

THE PRAIRIE

THE old surveyor's records told us little more about the tall-grass prairie than its extent and drainage patterns in the early 1800s, but there were other ways to find out about it. One was consulting the accounts of pioneer observers. Although finding trees for building cabins, barns, and fences was a problem, open grasslands were less depressing, to the womenfolk especially, than the gloom of dense forests. In 1833 young Judge Hugh McCulloch rode horseback through a prairie near LaPorte, Indiana, a town that took its name from the "door" where tree cover opened out into a vast expanse of tall grass:

> Its surface was undulating like the waves of the sea after a storm, and covered with luxurious grass interspersed with wild flowers of every hue. . . . I have seen since then many parks of great natural and artistic beauty, but none so charming as was the rolling prairie on the bright morning in June.

The prairie of history was made up, in its upper stratum, of tall-grass species; the plains country west of the prairie is short grass. The rough dividing line between the dominant species of the two types is the height of a man's waist. The prairie formed a rough equilateral triangle with its base running north-south along the 101st meridian near Dodge City, Kansas, narrowing eastward through Iowa and Missouri to an apex in northwestern Indiana. There were within it, to be sure, islands and interdigitation of forest, largely of the oak-hickory type, just as prairie patches were found within the forests of Indiana and even into Ohio.

This former prairie area might still be called tall grass today, since man's highly bred *Zea Mays* that has supplanted the native big bluestem is still a grass species. Cord grass grew tall in the wetter areas, and reed unfurled its flags to the wind where the land was still wetter but water was not deep enough for cattail and bulrush. On farm fields which were once prairie, the very deep, mellow, black topsoil extends over both low and high ground, whereas in fields that were originally forested the hollows are dark but the knolls and ridges have light brown soil.

The bamboo tree of the tropics is a member of the grass family. The tall grass of the prairie was no rival to bamboo, but in the wet prairies of Illinois and Indiana a tall man seated on a horse could tie the ends of the grass together over his head. Historians wrote that it was often so thick and tall as to hide a man riding a horse through it. A prairie fire whipped by a high wind was something to see—from a distance. This vegetation type was dependent less on climate than on recurrent fires caused by lightning or Indians, as was realized in 1816 by a visiting British botanist, David Thomas. Trees can grow throughout the tall-grass triangle area if protected from fire and other disturbance, for the climate is moist enough to support tree growth. This is not generally true in the short-grass area of the high plains west of the prairie.

A settler with an ordinary plow drawn by horses was not able to break the sod, because of the stout root systems of the great grasses. Virgin prairie was plowable only by itinerant "breaking teams" of eight oxen and two drivers, with a special, giant plow. Even with such equipment, a serious nuisance in prairie soil was the prevalence of "stool grubs" or underground trunks, often barrel-shaped, of prairie-edge trees like burr oak and black oak. The name was given them because, after stopping a plow cold, they had to be "grubbed" out by hand tools, and because, after a fire had killed back the upright, aboveground shoots, the grub would "stool out" with new leafy sprigs able to grow rapidly from the underground food storage. Most tree species, lacking this behavioral adaptation to prairie fires, were ruled out by never getting established in the first place.

In the Midwest of our own day, prairie is found only in a few small, protected pioneer cemeteries, in a few spots along railroad rights of way, and in odd corners. Preservation groups and government have done much better in saving forests than examples of prairie. In Indiana, only the Hoosier Prairie, just made a part of the national lakeshore in the Lake Michigan Dunes, is of fair size, being about 400 acres. Although the plants are real prairie species, the scene is not aesthetically pleasing since industry and railroads surround it. Illinois, having had much more prairie originally than Indiana, spent well over $2 million in 1967 for 1,400 acres of one tract, Goose Prairie, in the northeastern part of the state, and added much acreage later.

In the richest nation on earth, could not each prairie county in the Midwest have preserved a few hundred acres of original prairie sod untouched by the plow? Today's school children learning history, biology, or geography would have been able to swish through grasses taller than they and imagine how it was to ride the Conestoga wagons westward. Although it is generally agreed that money is a wonderful thing, it is sometimes possible to pay too high a price for it.

18

AN ELITE AND UNIQUE ALASKAN EXPEDITION

MANY expeditions to the ends of the earth have been remarkable, but none more so than the Harriman Alaska Expedition of 1899. Edward Henry Harriman (Averell's father) originally planned the trip as a family summer cruise and a hunt for the Alaskan Brown Bear, not yet bagged by a white man. Both these aims were fulfilled, but the voyage also developed into a primarily scientific venture when Harriman obtained Dr. C. Hart Merriam to recruit and head a scientific staff of extraordinary stature.

In the spring of 1899, Merriam was busy in his Washington office when an unexpected visitor appeared. This short, unassuming person said his name was Harriman and that he was a railroad man. The chief federal biologist was about to declare that he would not be interested in buying any excursion tickets, when Harriman went on to state that he was planning an expedition to Alaska in a couple of months and wanted Merriam to organize the scientific work. The biologist pointed out at once that the time was much too short to prepare an expedition for that same year, and that in any case the expense would be quite prohibitive. However, the visitor claimed that he had already chartered a ship and engaged officers and crew for a May 31 departure from Seattle.

In order to get the harmless crank out of his office, Merriam consented to talk with him at home that evening. Harriman left, and the mammalogist got back to work. Soon a thought struck him. He put on coat and hat, and walked to the nearest railroad company office. There he asked if they had ever heard of a railroad man named Harriman. "Yes, Mr. Edward Harriman of New York owns this company and controls a total of sixty thousand miles of track, plus a few steamship lines!"

Governor W. Averell Harriman, at our request, kindly wrote the following recollections of the expedition, for my *Bioscience* article which identifies the scientists in the group photograph.

> For a boy seven and one-half years old, the boarding of the steamship George W. Elder at Seattle for a voyage to the unknown north was an exciting experience. At that age one is apt to remember exciting experiences more than others, and the Harriman Alaska Expedition was filled with excitement.

> I recall steaming into the fiords with the great glaciers all around and hearing at intervals the boom from the icebergs breaking off. The trip up the newly built railroad to White Pass, and the many tragic stories of the Gold Rush miners attempting to climb their way to the upper reaches of the Yukon, is still indelible in my mind.

A particular thrill was being taken to the beach in Siberia in front of an Eskimo village. The Eskimos looked strange and formidable. But the greatest thrill of all was the night we hit a rock in the uncharted waters of the Bering Sea. It was about midnight. We were all pulled out of our bunks and told to put on our life jackets. When we came on deck, it was still broad daylight even at that hour at that latitude in June. The lifeboats were being prepared in case we had to abandon ship. I still vividly recall the thrill of thinking that we might have to put to sea in one of the lifeboats. I did not recognize any danger and thus had no fear. As it turned out, by reversing the propeller and other maneuverings, the captain was able to pull us off the rock, and we proceeded on our way.

Throughout the expedition the scientists talked freely with us children, and I remember particularly two men—John Burroughs and John Muir. They would walk the deck together and stop and talk to us in a kindly manner. This kindness tended to offset their rather terrifying appearance with their long gray beards.

Looking back it seems to me as if almost every day had some new and fascinating experience; so when we finally landed at Seattle two months later, I was a sad boy when I walked down the gangplank, thinking that the end had come. I had, of course, no conception of the lasting influence of the findings of the distinguished scientists who took advantage of the opportunity the trip afforded. In going to Alaska in recent years, I find that people still speak of the expedition and of the scientific discoveries that were made at that time.

Forty-two years later, the expedition came up in my first talk with Stalin. In September 1941, Lord Beaverbrook and I headed Anglo-American missions to Moscow to find out what supplies the Russians needed the most to help them hold out against the Hitler invasion. Stalin received us in the Kremlin on the first night of our arrival. He asked about my previous visits to Russia, and I told him that my first visit was made without a passport. He looked surprised. I explained that in 1899 my father had landed us on the east coast of Siberia, and of course we had no passports. He commented: "Oh, that was under the Czar; you couldn't do it now." He showed more concern with the security of Siberia than with my father's extraordinary expedition!

—W. AVERELL HARRIMAN
Washington, D.C.

The complement of 126 persons included the Harriman family and several guests, the officers and crew of the chartered vessel *George W. Elder*, and thirty top outdoor professionals from academia and government. Only one group photograph was taken of the key people. Its legend is merely "Who are we?" I largely answered this question, using many sources over a two-year period (See "Bioscience," June 1978).

John O' Mountains and John O' Birds, Muir and Burroughs, were the two outstanding literary naturalists of the day; both are included in Chapter 13 of the present book. Burroughs served as historian of the expedition, writing the popular narrative. The week the party spent at Glacier Bay was the fourth visit by Muir to the Muir Glacier over a twenty-year period. Glaciology was the field of science in which he made original contributions. The photographer Edward S. Curtis later became well-known for his superb life-work of forty thousand photographs of American Indians.

Dr. George Bird Grinnell, editor of *Forest and Stream*, had been a pupil of Audubon's widow Lucy, and a friend of her sons. He had founded the first Audubon Society thirteen years before the expedition, on which he was the anthropologist. He later conceived and pushed through the idea of our Glacier National Park, where a lake and a glacier are named for him. The forest expert of the party was E. B. Fernow, who had come from Europe to head the federal forestry program in the 1880s, before Gifford Pinchot. Frederick Dellenbaugh at age eighteen had been John Wesley Powell's artist and mapmaker during the second Colorado River Expedition, and later became a notable author and world traveler. Louis Agassiz Fuertes was one of several fine painters on the trip; he fell heir to the mantle of Audubon as a famed bird-artist. Most of the others on the staff were people whose names are still highly respected in their fields.

Like individuals, all expeditions make mistakes. The prize error perpetrated by this one was their regrettable and rather thorough looting of a "deserted" Indian village at Cape Fox. No mention of this incident has appeared in print before. Mrs. Mary Fuertes Boynton of Ithaca NY, whose father was Louis Agassiz Fuertes, wrote me as follows from Costa Rica on March 3, 1977.

> Thinking the Indian village abandoned, the party rushed off with all kinds of artifacts including [six huge] totem poles when as a matter of fact the Indians were simply away on a hunting trip. One of the stolen poles used to grace the Cornell campus until the days of Livingston Farrand who was a scholar of Indian cultures before he became President of Cornell University. He was so dismayed to see it that he had it moved to the Arnot Forest, where it is still standing.

The photograph standing at the head of this chapter was taken in this Indian village by Edward S. Curtis. My limerick about the mistake puts the situation succinctly:

The villagers called down a pox
On the scholarly looters at Fox,

> *Though that breach of their portal*
> *Made their culture immortal*
> *And taught them to utilize locks.*

Out of Seattle just two months, the party cruised nine thousand miles and touched Asia, visiting native villages, mission settlements, and tiny villages of white pioneers which grew into cities. That summer the Klondike gold rush was still going on, and from Skagway the party penetrated inland as far as the summit of White Pass, which was as far as the new railroad then extended, and saw many prospectors with back-breaking loads climbing to the pass, looking wistfully at the train which they could not afford to ride.

Extensive collections of plants and animals were taken back to museums and specialists, so that by 1901 thirteen new genera and more than six hundred species new to science had already been described. The chief geographic discovery, for which Edward Harriman was personally responsible, was the fifteen-miles Harriman Fiord and its five active glaciers. Amazingly, considering the mere two months in the field, the expedition's report filled fifteen large volumes, which Harriman financed and Merriam edited. The popular narrative by John Burroughs leads off the first volume, and that author published it also separately in his book *Far and Near*. The volumes contain many pen sketches made from the wealth of photographs taken; many paintings were reproduced as full-page color plates of a quality surprising for the 1901 publication. The Harrimans had gone north "loaded for bear" but actually bagged much bigger game—scientific immortality.

19

THE HARD NORTH COUNTREE

SINCE "geo" refers to Earth, Space is not a geographical frontier but an astronomical one. Alaska and the Northwest Territory of Canada were still the land frontiers of this continent when a bard wrote, "The North Countree is a hard countree, that mothers a bloody brood." That is no longer true, but the next line remains applicable: "And its icy arms hold hidden charms . . ." Although the literal frontier has passed away, this region is still inhabited by a disproportionate number of the earthy, resourceful pioneer type. The bush pilots who now make the hinterlands accessible to the rest of us are relics of the old, tough sourdough breed.

With a bush pilot who seemed to have a death-wish, engineer Robert Miles and I (who did not) flew in a small float plane northeastward from Yellowknife, Northwest Territories, into the arctic tundra near Lake Aylmer. It was the second field season of the Purdue Canadian Arctic Permafrost Expedition to survey terrain conditions in the Mackenzie Basin from Great Slave and Great Bear Lakes down the Mackenzie River to the Beaufort Sea and eastward from the extensive delta of that river. Aside from the flights from Chicago to Yellowknife, this was the first aerial work of our expedition in that year 1951. Patches of snow still held out in low, sheltered spots. The varied coloring of the tundra vegetation, from the gray of reindeer lichens, the light brown of peat mosses, through a range of yellows and greens, told us something about the underlying soil even from the air.

Our protracted approach to arctic timberline showed us a curious series of changing tree forms. While we were still over the spruce taiga, flying rather low in order to botanize visually, we saw that each tall tree had a small snow-mat where the lowest boughs were brighter green because the chronic snowcover of the long winter had shielded them from water-loss and wind damage. As we flew on, it became clear that the erect central trunks and their ordinary side branches were progressively shorter, while the low or prostrate snow-mats formed larger and larger discs at ground level. This trend continued with some regularity as the trees were seen closer and closer to arctic timberline. The last erect stems, though still recognizable as representing the main, original trunks, were spindling, near-leafless or even quite dead, a couple of feet tall and unbranched, and each emerged from the center of a deep-green, prosperous ground-cover about thirty feet in diameter, a far cry from the tall trees we had observed at the start. Both the low mat and its erect stick were parts of the same individual plant and had the same genetic make-up; this is an environmentally-induced difference. The north land is a hard place for trees as well as for people.

Finally it was threatening bad weather, and time to turn back. The bushie then explained that because an instrument was out of order he could not home in on the navigational beam from Yellowknife airstrip. After several hours of flying without recognizing any landmarks, or being able to raise the airstrip by two-way radio (also non-functional), twilight was approaching and it was raining, on the verge of snow. We decided to "land" the plane on a deep, narrow lake to spend the night. Because this lake, like most of them in the region, was very lovely, it was not unalloyed misery to sleep sitting up inside one's sleeping bag with clothes on, lulled to intermittent slumber in the never-dark, rainy night by the rocking of the plane. In the morning, we found that the rain had ceased but there was still a high overcast.

A practically dead battery made it quite difficult for the pilot, standing on a float to spin the propellor, to start the engine, but eventually we could lift off and head in the direction we hoped was toward Yellowknife. Since we had little idea where we were starting from, the compass was not very helpful. During this return leg of the flight we had time to contemplate how the lake vessel that had carried our gear north across Great Slave had returned southward with a new widow returning to Ontario. It was heartbreaking to glimpse a dead flyer's survivor in tears as she looked back at the town while the ship pulled away. The search for her husband by several big Canadian government search planes had been abandoned after three fruitless weeks and expenditure of several hundred thousands of dollars. A bush plane, regardless of color, is an almost impossibly minute object to be sighted in the limitless, monotonous expanse at the top of the continent.

Our gasoline supply was running dangerously low because the service mechanic at the airstrip had disregarded our pilot's order to fill the supplementary tanks, and the bushie had neglected to check them. For two eternities, one apiece, Prof. Miles and I held the large maps across our laps, carefully comparing the form of any distinctive lake beneath and around the plane's course with the shapes shown in blue on the maps. This should have been a good idea, but it did not seem to be working. The gas was now really low and we began to wonder about our prospects, or lack of them, for a safe dead-stick landing.

Through a sudden revelation, we could point out to the pilot a lake of unusual outline both on the map and on the earth, which gave us the providential bearing on Yellowknife. After a time, approaching it but still from some distance away, the needle indicated perhaps as much as two gallons of remaining gas. We made it to the airport and landed on the nearby water. The plane eased to the dock.

While I was kissing the ground, Bob, the practical engineer, asked the pilot to check the tank. He found a dip-stick, took off the cap, and carefully investigated, but offered no information. "Well," asked Miles, "What's left there?" The pilot then spoke one vibrant and eloquent word: "Vapor!"

Perhaps the difficulties we had encountered bore some relationship to a fact observed later at the Yellowknife City Dump where I went to see ravens at close range. At least 80 per cent of the contributions seen there consisted of a colossal pile of empty liquor bottles glinting cheerfully in the midnight sun.

For the next flight we chartered a different plane to take us up the main or northeast arm of Great Slave Lake. I arranged to be left alone on huge, uninhabited Et Then Island, to spend three days collecting plant specimens during a solitary hike to the other end of the island. At bedtime the second night, on crawling into the alpine tent and removing my heavy socks, I was dismayed at the appearance of my calves. They were thickly studded with tufts of a gray fungus, like a plant of the bread mold (*Rhizopus*) magnified several hundredfold. An attack of tropical rot just below the arctic circle? At least it was not causing any pain except a mental one from lack of a diagnosis.

After a little anguished thought I hit precisely upon the etiology of this infestation. When I had been dressing outdoors the previous morning, black flies rising in clouds from the deep moss had bitten my bare legs voraciously, and a little drop of lymph had exuded from each bite. After I pulled on the wool socks this liquid dried down, gluing some gray fibers of wool at the point of each bite. When the socks were next removed, a fluffy bit of wool remained, radiating away from the bite site like oversized hyphae of some carnivorous fungus.

The high plateau of Et Then Island is bordered by a steep escarpment, broken down in six places by embayments, the slopes of which are generally gradual and made of small boulders. On the full length of each bay slope is a series of rock terraces called beach ridges because each level of the stepwise formation was once lapped by lake water. The oldest of these beach levels is the highest, six hundred feet above the present lake level, whereas the youngest of them is still being formed by ice-shove and wave action along the present shore.

This high island of today was completely submerged only 8,000 or fewer years ago. The meltwaters from the thawing continental ice sheet were then much higher and covered much more area horizontally than the present Great Slave Lake, huge as this is. It was not as much as six hundred feet higher in absolute measure, for geologists are sure that there has not only been an absolute lowering and shrinking of the old lake (as glacial Lake Chicago also changed to form the much smaller Lake Michigan), but that the earth's crust has also arched upward considerably as it was relieved of the weight of the glacier.

In flying around the island later to photograph this unusual display of beach ridges, accentuated by differing plant cover on the ridges from that in the troughs between, I was better able to appreciate the uniqueness of this scene. Ordinarily, the changes that we see or infer in land surfaces are very small-scale ones caused by water's erosion or deposition, by wind, gravity, glaciers or lava flows. Here at Et Then, however, one saw clear evidence of very recent, large-scale movements of the Earth's crust itself.

While boating the full length of the world's twelfth longest river to the Mackenzie Delta and the Arctic Sea, we often took a small outboard craft to explore the clear, shallow tributary streams. In many places along them, where the stream had cut sections in muskegs and bogs, an undercut root-mat hung down from the top edge of the cut bank as crenulated festoons of live roots and dark, peaty organic matter. Water usually dripped from these heavy drapes, derived from the horizontal bog-blotter farther inland. This sight is common along subarctic streams; I never saw anything like it farther south. The hanging curtains are opaque to light and excellent insulators against heat transfer into the permafrost that underlies the muskeg deposit.

Once when I noted glints of light coming from the gloom behind a vertical peat-mat, I beached the small boat, climbed the sandslope, and ducked into the narrow space behind the dripping curtain. With eyes adjusting to the gloom, I was looking, to my amazement, through a clear, vertical or slightly inward-curving wall of ice five feet high and sixty feet long.

It was a vertical section of a pond, not of liquid water but of transparent ice. One can imagine a museum habitat group of a winter pool, as one looked at it edgewise from a point lower than its surface. But instead of having been turned to ice a few years or decades ago, this had been solid ice for many millennia. I was gazing, most likely, into a Pleistocene aquatic landscape, quite undisturbed since the end of the glacial epoch when water from the thawing ice sheet had suddenly been refrozen as it lay, from top to bottom, by a sudden cold snap. The original green of the leaves of waterweeds and moss was now brown, for we expect sepia tones in old pictures. Twigs and partly decayed sticks were there within arm's reach except that a medium where man is unwelcome was protecting them. It would look the same in a winter pond of today if completely frozen, except for what people would have thrown into it. Preserved in ice of uniform, crystal clarity, it appeared to have been quickly embedded in clear plastic for display in perpetuity.

The temperature that made me shiver was fossilized cold from the Ice Age. This involuntary dance of my muscles was the same as my not very remote ancestors had experienced along the edge of the European continental glacier; their culture and physical evolution, and consequently my own, had been conditioned by cold such as I was feeling—come down through a lapse of time in which all of what we call civilization had been produced.

Placing a hand on the cold, wet wall of ancient ice, I was glad not to be on the other side, trapped like an unwary mastodon behind that interface where past and present meet. After a final incredulous look, I was satisfied to return to the comforting sunlight of a summer day in our own current interglacial period.

20

SETTING THE COURSE FOR ALASKA

THE Alaska Highway stretches 1,520 miles from Dawson Creek, Canada, to Fairbanks, Alaska. Four-fifths of its length is in Canada, and only the first ninety miles of that was paved. While today the highway is well maintained, it was heavily overloaded, during the period of pipeline construction, by U. S. tourists and firms who got most of the use from it but paid nothing toward its maintenance. When it was dry, the big trucks zooming past our Suburban truck and trailer raised clouds of dust that dangerously obscured oncoming traffic. After sprinkler trucks wetted it down to lay the dust, driving was safer but dirtier from spattering mud. Windshields and windows had to be specially shielded against gravel thrown up by passing trucks. We had seven tires punctured by sharp rocks. Between our northward and southward trips three months apart in 1975, we fortunately missed the effect of one tremendous washout, which no vehicle could pass in either direction for three weeks of the brief summer season. Although the guide-books state that the Alaska Highway is a permanent monument to the friendship between two great nations, it seemed to us at the time that it was Canada's revenge for the United States having pulled out of the British Empire.

On a sweeping curve of a remote section of road, which had just been wetted down, I failed to realize at first that the sprinkler truck, returning empty, was on our side of the road. Surely the driver would pull over as soon as he saw us. No such thing—he came on without slackening speed. No use for me to pull over to my wrong side, he might too. At the very last moment, I pulled hard over to our right into the soft, soaking berm. He never slowed, never deviated from the middle of my lane, and missed our trailer's left rear corner by less than a foot. Evidently he would have deliberately collided with our Suburban truck; I had been almost too trusting and too slow to prevent it. He disappeared up the road, still on my side, without an apologetic toot. Both my vehicles were mired a foot deep in soft wet clay; only by getting out in it to activate the four-wheel drive was I finally able, in the lowest low gear, to maneuver onto the remote stretch of road again.

We are still puzzled by this incident—one of the "strange things done in the midnight sun." Perhaps that bored truck-driver enjoyed terrifying American motorists with his thrilling game of "chicken."

Because my wife had never seen arctic tundra and I had not seen the Brooks Range, we took a scheduled flight from Fairbanks to Bettles within the Arctic Circle. Much of the plane's route followed the pipeline's course, and we could see from the air why the plan had disturbed environmentalists. An incredible aggregate area of tundra was disrupted, with pipeline and surface road rights of way, and side roads to numerous camps, staging and storage areas, and airstrips.

The original agreement between the oil consortium and the state was for the former to build a state highway along the course eventually, but sober second thoughts have intervened. If there were such a road open to tourists and hunters, it would soon become merely the midrib of a pinnately-veined leaf of road system and tundra terrain. A vast expanse of tundra, after disturbance by vehicles and unable to recover in terms of a human life span, would be threaded by jeep roads far to both sides of the main road, like the many lateral veins of a metaphorical leaf. One object of our flight to Bettles was to get aerial color shots of the variegated, colorful tundra before that could happen.

The Eskimos and Indians at Bettles seemed nonplussed by the current activity. An Indian told us that the closer you look into things that man has made the uglier they become, but the closer you examine Nature's things the more beautiful they are. A perceptive conclusion to come from someone who had never seen a microscope! Nothing appears disgusting when seen through that instrument.

Many of the passengers to the tundra were young people coming for canoe float-trips on the Koyukuk River, or for backpacking excursions. Each year the scarcity value of natural solitude increases as the supply diminishes. During a backpacking trip, the mate and I had seen no one on the trail all day. Toward sundown, while threading the shoreline of an isolated lake, we noted a young fellow sitting alone at the water's edge across a narrow bay. He did not see us, so my sociable wife called across to him. Startled, he spotted us and called back, "What's that again?"

Now embarrassed at breaking the spell of evening, nevertheless she was trapped into raising her voice in a near shout, and repeating, "You know where to find solitude, don't you?" The stranger thought for a moment, then bellowed back, "I'm afraid not!"

The year 1975 was one when the "second gold rush" was in progress—the long-awaited effort to settle into an equitable division of Alaskan lands and resources among the Native Peoples, the State, the Great White Father, and private commercial interests. Prevalent attitudes were crystallizing toward legal actions which would determine the fate of the region for the long future.

The two kinds of men we found in Alaska that year were the tatooed and the untatooed. Pipeline construction was bringing in many more of the former. Among these were many born-again hunters, including ones who were not also wildlife conservationists. Many Alaskans saw the importance of protecting subsistence hunting by the natives, and this was finally allowed even in the new national parks and preserves, although hunting organizations opposed it. Other Alaskans were demanding an unrealistically loose policy regarding resources on federal lands, not admitting that "This land belongs to you and me." It was therefore very refreshing to get acquainted with James and Nancy Barlow and to be their enthralled guests for two days in their remote log-cabin homestead on a wilderness lake. Jim stands six feet seven inches, and hails from the town in New Jersey where my wife grew up. Mrs. Barlow is a nurse from New Zealand, a country I love from two visits and some mountaineering. They met when he was in that country on the way back from the antarctic expedition from Ohio State University which discovered the first amphibian fossil on the Antarctic Continent, one four feet long.

Jim holds distinguished mountain-climbing records on Mount McKinley (Denali), and serves in rescue work there on occasion. Dr. Bradford Washburn, the authority on Mount McKinley, termed "extraordinary" the East-West traverse of Mount McKinley and Mount Hunter in 1963, by Jim and three companions, which surmounted both North and South Peaks. In 1967, Jim and two different companions made the first winter ascent of Mount McKinley. I found we had one more modest climbing experience in common, the ascent of Mount Rainier.

Jim is not one of the tatooed persuasion, nor does he countenance playing a game of "chicken" with Alaska's natural beauty and publicly-owned resources. The people this couple know best are old-line Alaskans who supported the Alaska Coalition of about twenty conservation organizations which worked for nine years to get it done right this time, and in 1980 triumphed by the skin of their teeth. We told Jim and Nancy about our friends Margaret and Louise Murie, of Moose, Wyoming, who were writing and working for the same cause. They are half-sisters born in Alaska who married the half-brothers Olaus and Adolph Murie, men who have never been surpassed as field naturalists in Alaska.

Jim and Nancy built the two-story log cabin, with a lakeside sauna and other log outbuildings, where mighty Denali gleams (weather permitting, of course) across their private lake not forty miles distant, which is very close for a peak more than twenty-thousand feet high. Their site can be reached only by two miles of inconspicuous, overgrown foot-trail. All the logs he cut were from spruce trees which grew at least a half-mile from the cabin or lake, and were spaced so that no stump can be seen from any other stump. For fuel-wood he takes only defective trees, or too-crowded ones, and digs the earth away from the base so as to leave no stump. All this speaks eloquently for Jim's environmental beliefs; his muscles back up his convictions and his talk. To keep their trail unworn, heavy supplies are brought in only over winter snows. When snow is gone, only what fits into back-packs is brought in.

Nancy teaches their three children by correspondence courses. Jim makes the living by harvesting one moose each year, working at a job six months a year, and gardening in the side yard by the lake. His job is a highly responsible, but seasonal, conservation post. Their neighbors are distant in terms of miles, but close otherwise. They respect other people's choice of life-style, but still consider that their way of life is the best one for them.

During the years shortly before the 1980 National Interest Lands Conservation Act, when there was, ludicrously, only one national park in all of Alaska, Jim Barlow was certainly a wallflower at what he felt was an orgy of quick-and-dirty development of Alaska.

21

THE STATESMAN AND THE SKULL

A STRIKING case of overthrust-fault geology is the eastern flank of our Rockies, the Lewis Range. There, in Montana's Glacier National Park, at the farthest edge of the massive earth block which was shoved eastward from the elongated break, the tooth of Time has left but one spectacular, isolated remnant of the moved block, famed Chief Mountain, intruding into the high plains country.

On the precipitous east face of the Chief, where the motorist on the road to Canada can clearly see it, the effect of the tremendous Lewis Overthrust is evident: the old pre-Cambrian rocks rest *on top of* the younger Cretaceous strata of the plain. This significant line of division lies just above the talus slope under the towering cliff. The plains east of the Rockies have short-grass vegetation because of the dry climate in the rain-shadow of the mountains. The forest on the south slope of Chief Mountain burned in 1935 from an escaped campfire, and the trees have found too little moisture for fast regeneration.

Mount Stimson, at the head of Nyack Creek in the park, was named for Henry L. Stimson, one of the number of highly educated amateur naturalists, hunters, and anthropology hobbyists who delighted in the barbarous West of their day. George Bird Grinnell, Theodore Roosevelt, and Stimson were among such outdoorsmen. The latter served as the Secretary of State under Hoover, and of War under Taft and again for World War II.

In 1891 young Stimson, with his physician friend Walter James, made the first ascent of Chief Mountain by white men. They climbed the most difficult way, by the sheer east face. Their guide was Indian Billy, a Piegan Blackfoot. Stimson's account of the climb is in a rare 1895 publication of the Boone and Crockett Club. "Down deep in our hearts, battling with the awe we felt for him, was the almost unspoken hope that perhaps in some way we might struggle up his sheer sides and make him, in a way he was to no one else, our king."

Stimson, who had spent several summers in the region, was satisfied that no Piegan Blackfoot had ever climbed the Chief. But these Indians had heard an old legend from the Flatheads across the range. It averred that, many, many years before, a great chief had told on his death-bed that as a youth seeking his vision which would protect and guide him through adult life he had carried a sacred buffalo skull to the summit of Chief Mountain. He spent four days and nights there, fasting, and used the skull as a pillow. He experienced his sacred visions, and left the skull up there.

The Stimson party had a long and arduous trip merely packing to the Chief's base. One of the white men dropped out early in the climb. After a number of difficulties and some hair-raising experiences on the east precipice, Stimson, James, and the Blackfoot guide made it to the summit at 1:30.

We pushed our way carefully along to the highest point of the narrow ridge. . . . Just as we reached it, Indian Billy, who was in the lead, suddenly stopped and pointed to the ground. There, on the very summit of Chief Mountain, safely anchored by rocks from the effect of wind or tempest, lay a small, weather-beaten bison skull. It was certainly one of the very oldest I have ever seen. Even in the pure air of that mountain top it had rotted away until there was little else than the frontal bone and the stubs on which had been the horns. Billy picked it up and handed it to us quietly, saying with perfect conviction, "The old Flathead's pillow." We left the skull where it had been found. . . . We shared his reverence too much to allow us to remove its offering.

There is a sequel to this true story. In the *Lethbridge Herald* for July 16, 1947, F. H. Rigall wrote thus of a letter he received from Secretary Stimson in the U. S. War Office.

Many years after his first ascent the Colonel revisited his old stamping ground. . . . One evening he was wandering alone around the base of the rocky crown of Chief Mountain [presumably not the difficult east face this time] and upon rounding a corner of the rocks came upon two young fellows of the college student type, who were in the act of coiling up a climbing rope and stowing it in a rucksack, evidently having just made the descent of the mountain. The Colonel introduced himself to the climbers and related the account of his own ascent, so many years before. The young men were naturally very interested in comparing routes and experiences, but as the story progressed to the finding of the buffalo relic they began to show unmistakable signs of acute embarrassment, and upon conclusion of the Colonel's narrative they shamefacedly produced, from the depths of the rucksack, the identical fragment of bone!

They explained that, not knowing its historical significance, they had taken it as a souvenir of their climb. Only a few moments of discussion were necessary for all to agree that to rifle the cairn of its treasure would be a shocking act of vandalism, not to be considered for a moment. The upshot of the matter was that all three re-ascended the mountain and very carefully replaced the skull in its original resting place! A note was also left with it in a small can giving a brief account of the origin of the skull and begging subsequent climbers to respect its hoary antiquity and allow it to remain in peace where the young Kootenaie of the olden times had dreamed his dream and seen his visions in the long, long ago.

22

GOBLIN GOLD

THE visitor was over eighty and wise in the ways of the Maine coast. I was a third as old and a newcomer there. She had wondered about "goblin gold" since early girlhood, and wanted to get it straight in her mind before leaving this world of strange things. Having heard that a young ecologist was teaching teachers at the first Audubon Nature Camp for Adult Leaders, she rowed out on Muscongus Bay to our island.

I was completely mystified by her description of the caverns with their bright store of gold which vanished on closer approach. So we set a date when we would go together to the seaward slope on the farm where she was born and brought up.

We looked into the entrances of several small caves on

that wooded hillside of her home place. Each cavern floor displayed a flat carpet, wall to wall and brighter than bullion, for it appeared like a sheet of stained glass transmitting light from beneath it to pass through as a living greenish-gold hue. We seemed not to be seeing a material by reflected light, but to be looking into a direct source of light itself under the cavern floor. But after stepping into the cave to look for a cause, we could see no more of that color and brightness. It had turned into a commonplace floor of moist brown soil and nothing more. The gold had become a very recent memory as impalpable as the tail of a comet.

With a knife blade I shaved off a thin layer of the dull surface soil and took it away in a vial of alcohol. Having no microscope in camp, I sent the preserved soil to the Smithsonian, and anxiously awaited their analysis. Would it prove to be some ethereal phenomenon of biology, or of mineralogy, or perhaps mere illusion stemming from imperfections of eye or mind in confronting the unknown?

Word came back that the effect of molten gold was caused by the threads (protonema) of the rare cave moss, *Schistostegia*, growing invisibly over and among the soil particles. In any moss species, the tiny spore grows into a horizontal mat of threads, microscopic in size; later this normally gives rise to the erect, green stage. This is the familiar, mature moss "plant." No other kind of moss produces the reflection effect we saw. Each thread of the cave moss is made up of rounded cells attached end to end in single file like a filamentous green alga. In the dim light where it alone can grow, the cells can obtain enough light for photosynthesis only by having a very special adaptation.

The problem is solved by having the curved cell-wall that faces the cave entrance bend the light rays so as to *concentrate* or almost point-focus them upon the few small chloroplasts, all lying against the far wall. The red and blue wavelengths, of course, were absorbed for their energy. The useless greenish-yellow light (the color of the chloroplast bodies) was reflected back from the chloroplasts, and again refracted by the cell wall acting like the lens of a flashlight aimed out of the cave. However, when the observer's eye moves in any direction away from the line of that light beam, the golden glow disappears. The phantom gold, like other wonders of the natural world, eludes the person who would reduce it to his possession.

The next and only other time I saw the cave moss was in Michigan during a week-long field trip of the botanical society. We were led to the shallow cave by Dr. Elzada Clover, one of the first two women, both midwestern professors of botany, who ran the Colorado River through the Grand Canyon.

Thus, I was preconditioned to recognize, a decade later, the nature of a still more remarkable optical effect that *was* totally new to science. This was to prove the most original specific find I made in a long career in ecology.

The most familiar of all recent lava beds, on this continent at least, lies athwart Interstate 40, old US 66, the Santa Fe Railroad main line, and the air routes into Los Angeles from the east. El Malpais, near Grants, New Mexico, is where I studied plant and animal life on and off between 1944 and 1948, and returned in 1981 to rephotograph three hundred precise sites for the federal Bureau of Land Management.

When molten lava spreads out from volcanic vents and its surface first cools and solidifies, deeper molten streams continue to flow. Their red-hot, hidden portions still run downstream beneath the surface crust, leaving behind hollow channels up to a hundred feet in width. At points where their thin ceilings collapse, the tube cave is opened to the surface as gullies, or sinkholes great and small. The Grants lava bed is unique in that groundwater is abundant in the body of the malpais; hence, one may find a range of sinks from hidden pits with sunken gardens of rare ferns to large open sinks with marsh vegetation.

Standing at the bottom of a natural entrance ramp of fallen

roof-rocks, I was looking into a cave that had a crescentic pool well back beneath an overhanging roof. As my eyes became adjusted to the dimmer light I delightedly recognized an ephemeral golden gleam like those shown to me years before by two memorable old ladies—one had been a Maine coast mermaid and the other a canyon queen.

The closer I approached on the line of incident light, the brighter the floating gold dust appeared, like direct light coming through a huge color transparency. But as I moved sidewise from that central line, the glow soon disappeared, leaving a barely-visible, dull grayish film, like a dead television screen, on the water. Cave moss could not be growing on or in water—perhaps some sort of unseen floating alga was behind this mystery.

A search of books and journals revealed that such an effect in water had never been made known, and I embarked on a study to understand its mechanism. Experts on algae identified the floating "bloom" as composed of the single cells of the microscopic alga *Chlorella*. The two species causing the phantom color there are spherical cells only one twenty-five hundredths of an inch in diameter. They have no "tail" or other organ for moving the cell as a whole, but the living contents can shift around inside the extremely thin cellulose wall. Plant physiologists have long been familiar with the plant under other circumstances, especially in laboratory cultures for research in nutrition.

Now I had to dream up experiments and observations suitable for unraveling the mysterious effect, and study it at all seasons and different times of day and different sizes of cave opening. By building a wooden floor over the dry part of the cave's bottom, I could do detailed work by microscope, camera, and optical density measurements on the negative rolls, at different angles of deviation from the central axis of incoming light. The results were brought out in the journal *Ecology* in 1949.

Only one explanation fulfilled the conditions of the long-term experimentation. In reasonably good light, when the thin floating bloom looked gray, the green chloroplast bodies within the cell were facing every which way, producing no interesting color or reflection. In the dark of night, too, the cells never show consistent orientation of the living contents, nor do they during the first fifteen minutes after I stirred or mixed, or merely blew air from a medicine-dropper on the surface bloom.

However, when the undisturbed bloom is in dim light coming from one direction, the contents are so placed within the walls as to keep the chloroplast on the side away from the light. The curved outer parts nearest the light act as a lens, concentrating light to a near-focus upon the chloroplast, and unused light (gold in summer and greenish-gold in winter) is sent back, straight along the central line again, to the observer. But a person standing outside the narrow cone of reflected remnant-light can see at most a delicate grayish scum.

Thus is light, too dim for photosynthesis in ordinary plants, made usable by an amazing adaptation, for the minute cell-lenses are not below the surface film of pond water, but floating upon the water meniscus. Thus, light strikes through air directly into the cell. The extraordinary thing about this newer sort of goblin gold is that an effect requiring the cells to become and remain properly oriented internally is produced by a film of individual, unconnected cells floating upon the water, not at all in the water. It can only take place in a very special habitat where and when dim light comes from one direction and no wind or water currents disturb the way the cells lie facing the light. Nature, abhoring a vacuum, has found a way for some light-using plants to grow where none would be expected.

One night while climbing out of the best *Chlorella* cavern I was riveted by a strange sound coming out of the darkness over the black, lonely malpais. It was coming from a long way off, perhaps just an unusual effect of the night wind. I turned off the flashlight and stood still. The sound built or wavered as the wind waned or gusted, seeming the wildest and scariest ululation I had ever heard, and utterly appropriate to the surroundings. Although reminiscent of very distant singing of a coyote pack, it could hardly have been that exactly.

That long, low tongue of lava is within the Acoma Indian Reservation. The next day an Indian friend told me what had made the wailing that I thought symbolized the desert wilderness in the night. A crew of Navajo workmen employed to keep up the Santa Fe tracks were camped somewhere nearby. I had barely heard their immemorial tribal chants, distorted by distance and wind, calling up the unseen dark spirits of the malpais vastness.

23

THE INS AND OUTS OF ICE CAVES

UNLIKE many of our western mountains, the ancient Adirondacks were not hammered out on the anvil of Vulcan. Yet Charles Carroll, the innkeeper at Chimney Mountain Lodge and an amateur geologist, believed that Chimney Mountain is volcanic and that the precipitous rift at its summit is a remnant crater. Geologists tell us differently today, but when Charles was leading two others down a rope into a narrow, three-hundred foot shaft, we thought we were exploring a volcanic crater. Charles had discovered the cave two months earlier, and we were the next ones to enter it.

Hand over hand, feet pushing against the rock walls, we descended the rope. Lateral tunnels beckoned outward, and we investigated them. At the deepest point we could reach, the space widened out considerably. Our flashlights revealed an ice cascade, broad and steep. Its slope led the flashlight beams down beyond our vision.

Charles dislodged a loose boulder from the cavern wall. Big as a medicine ball, it slid rapidly down the icy chute, its loud noise reverberating back up to us. We listened for it to stop abruptly when it hit some bottom. Instead, the roaring sound gradually faded until dead silence filled our underworld. To leave no doubt of what we had experienced, Charles released another boulder to the slide, and then a third. His personal ice cave is not only deep; for practical speleological purposes it seemed bottomless. Hang on now! Let's not go tobogganing down a subterranean glacier, within instead of upon a mountain, toward an endless, black, frigid Hades where gravity plays the Mephistophelian role.

That Chimney Mountain abyss is the only ice cave I know which is not of volcanic origin. The many others I have seen are in lava flows. The black malpais rock with its many air-bubbles is year-round insulation against loss of the coolness from winter snow-packs, heavily sinking cold air, and the resulting ice. I have been in such cold sinks in California lava flows, and in a third of the thirty or more known ice caves seven thousand feet above sea level in El Malpais, New Mexico. Some of these I studied in some detail, along with the surface ecology of this 220-square-mile volcanic wilderness.

One ice cave there is open to the public, and managed by the proprietors of the Ice Caves Trading Post, who built a flight of wooden steps for ease and safety. At the bottom, there is a flat floor of ice of unknown depth, and beyond it rears a high mass of ice with a vertical edge or ice-wall facing the entrance ramp and stairs. This wall was fourteen feet high in 1926, nine feet in 1945, and down to four in 1981.

Growing directly on the dimly-lit face of this ice are two species of the blue-green alga *Stichococcus*, tinting the ice-wall green. Nowhere else had this genus been found growing on ice or snow before, except for a 1908 collection of it from Antarctica. The flat ice of the cavern floor is made bright green by *Sphaerella lacustris*, which had never before been found growing on ice or snow anywhere.

Another ice cave nearby, at 7,800 feet elevation also, has its own distinction. Within its cool, north-facing entrance I collected the first North American specimens of the arctic-alpine moss *Homomallium incurvatum*. This appears to be the first case on record in which climatic compensation is afforded a far-northern plant by an ice-cave situation or any habitat other than very high altitude.

One most unusual ice-cave near there, but not on any trail, has a rock-ramp that slopes gently southward into the north-facing cave entrance where direct sunlight never strikes. Below the ponderosa pine forest around the sink, I had to traverse eight other distinct zones of vegetation in climbing down the ramp. Beyond the last belt of land plants, the cave mouth was occluded completely by a pond of ice-water a foot deep over a mass of solid ice. By setting up a microscope at the water's edge, I learned that, in summer, living animalcules were swarming just where the water overlay the ice, where the temperature was right at the freezing point. Once on starting down into this sink, I scared up a wildcat. It bounded up from the cold pool where it had been drinking, and away through the pines above.

In the cool, moist, ever-shaded cave mouth was a band of the liverwort *Marchantia* on the rocks, and next below it a belt with two species of moss that were new to New Mexico. More remarkable, lower down and to the water's edge where July-August temperatures ranged only between 33.3 to 34.9° F., a new discovery awaited. The plant community there consisted of the moss *Pohlia cruda*, which occurs from the far north to the tropics. However, in this one known site, it is not the familiar, erect, leafy (gametophyte) plant that dominates, although a very few occur and make identification possible. It is a community of *protonemal threads* that dominates over the black soil near the cold water. The protonema, normally seen only under a microscope, is the first stage of moss growth after the spore germinates. Unprecedented as a stand visible to the naked eye, the green threads here had woven themselves into a velvet-like layer over the soil. The protonema had reversed roles with the "normal," upright green plant and become the long-lived, propagative, dominant phase of the life cycle. Evidently it tolerates the growth-season cold much better, not only than the later mature stage of the same species, but better than any stage of any other moss species that grows in higher, warmer parts of this cave entrance.

In the mid-Forties one could not get into this cave beyond the above-described plug of ice. By 1981, however, the ice had receded so that with four young men of the Bureau of Land Management we entered the depths by rope, past a slide of ice coating the steep part of the floor. Deep in the dark we found a deposit of man-made charcoal twenty-five feet along the cave and two feet deep, and potsherds with the clay still remembering the potters' hands. There were animal bones, and bones probably human. It was evident that the known warm period from 900 to 1300 A.D. was a time of Indian occupancy in this general area, ended by a cold time thereafter when the ice plug denied further access until sometime after I first saw it thus in the early Forties.

A spring day in 1981 on the lava surface turned into a seasonless night of constant chill as we pushed beyond the icy flooring, into a narrowing passageway. A slim spelunker we call "Buzz" was leading our gang of four; he was the most experienced. He squirmed along in a tight spot with the thought that the passage would widen further on. Next we wondered why he had come to a stop in his crawl. He reported calmly that his hard-hat was stuck and he had no room to reach a hand forward to loosen the chin strap. No help could come past his body from others, and no one was ahead of him to unwedge his hard-hat with a backward kick. The Stygian blackness ahead must have presaged to him the dark finality. Buzz had got himself into a predicament where all the King's horses and men were unavailing.

Was he recalling the news accounts of cave accidents he

had read over the years? Did his loved ones and the high-spots of his life file through his mind in an unbidden funeral march? Tight imprisonment in a rocky sepulchre must soon bring accelerating waves of claustrophobic panic like a night hurricane's surf surging against sea cliffs.

Not at all! Buzz lay quietly resting while he figured the angles. He knew that he must, before his strength left him, yank back forcefully and at exactly 180° on each azimuth from the direction his hat had entered the rock constriction. After half an hour of calm thought and alternating bursts of intense effort he succeeded in doing just that, and was free.

24

THE LAST OF THE OLD GUNFIGHTERS

IN New Mexico, on a June day in 1981, two things happened to me—one modern and the other old-fashioned, but both outside my previous experience. Two television stations sent helicopters with camera crews out to a lava wilderness to cover my resumption of an ecological project I had started thirty-seven years before. The more novel event was making the acquaintance of a rare man who has nearly ninety years of wild west life in his memory.

During previous days of field work with a man from the U. S. Bureau of Land Management, he told me of long talks about the old days with a former U. S. Marshall who still dresses like one and wears a big star. Let us call him Jake Grimes, to protect the more or less innocent.

After the TV interviewers had flown back to edit the tapes for that evening's and the next morning's news broadcasts, and we had driven from Old Woman Rock through a furious hailstrom that thickly covered the road with ice, we stopped at a carbon-copy Stuckeys beside an interstate highway. Just as my friend was about to phone in his report of the day's work, a battered jeep stopped out front and a spry old man got out, dressed in authentically dirty Old West fashion and packing a holstered .45 on his lean hip. I nudged my companion and whispered, "There's another one!" But he replied with suppressed excitement, "No, that's Jake himself." I should have known he would be one of a kind. Our introductions started an hour-long, stand-up reminiscence outside the roadhouse.

Jake wears a Spanish-style, flat-brimmed black hat, with

raven's tail feathers stuck in the rim. The hat folds down the top edges of his long ears. A grease-blackened leather vest is so short that it could not obstruct a quick draw of his loaded pistol. Throughout his low, mumbling monologue, laced with both sincere religious exhortations and profanity, he pulled at his straggly, grizzled beard. Like a disproportionate number of the cowboy types of his day, he was a Southerner, having been born in Virginia. Pinned to his shirt is a Deputy Sheriff's star which has been out of force for years. There is considerable popular sentiment for taking his six-gun and star away from him, but no volunteers have come forward.

Jake claimed that early in the century he accompanied Theodore Roosevelt on a hunt. TR wanted young eagles to donate to a zoo, and asked Jake to climb a cliff to the nest. Jake brought down two well-advanced eaglets in good condition, for which Roosevelt paid him $30.

He rambled on about his dislike of Pinkerton detectives, and how he once had to shoot one dead in the line of duty. His monotone made it seem that he thought all his dramatic exploits were commonplace, barely worth mentioning. He himself had served time for shooting a man in 1970. When my friend asked how many men he had killed in all, Jake replied that he could remember only thirty-two of them. In local legend, that is regarded as a wildly conservative figure. It is generally believed that he allows no one to touch him, but he shook hands vigorously with us at the end of our talk.

Because of his reputation, his arsenal, and a dog with a wolf's personality, people consider it risky to approach his home, even in broad daylight. His few friends think all this security is justified because he knows too much about too many people, some of whom are back in circulation and not grateful to him. Although the most outrageous stories about Jake are current, they seem to be, largely at least, fabrications. His own accounts of his career seem reasonable, though there is a slight fuzziness about the year some events occurred.

Throughout our long talk, Mrs. Grimes waited in the jeep. She carried a revolver on her hip, a shotgun across her lap, and a rifle was racked across the rear window. The Grimes are a couple after the heart of the National Rifle Association. The jeep was obstructing access to the self-service pumps, but everyone who bought gas for more than an hour seemed to prefer full service.

It is refreshing to encounter the real thing in this age of the rhinestone urban cowboy. One wonders, however, why Jake cannot conform, wear inconspicuous clothes, and relinquish his gun and star? My guess, based on knowing him for only an hour, is that his get-up represents a defiant nose-thumbing at today and its inhabitants. He seems to be telling us that the world has changed but he has not and doesn't intend to. He believes in his old self, seeing no need to adapt to an inferior new world filled too full of inferior new people. Though his six-shooter is now mainly a symbol, Jake is as much a fighter as he ever was, but in a losing cause.

Possibly the last of the High Noon gunmen, he is frontier history incarnate—the history of a people as rugged, uncultivated, and dangerous as the dark malpais along the continental divide nearby. We have commercialized and sentimentalized this passionate, often sordid, sometimes heroic history into the American mythology. As long as Jake survives, and a few others like him if there be any, the primitive and violent Old West will not have completely passed into legend.

25

THE HOUSE THAT GRASS BUILT

"I BUILD my house natural, out of earth and grass, like the world is made." So said a Spanish-American in a village along the Rio Grande as he set another terron into the wall of his new home.

When I found no one in the University of New Mexico who could tell me anything not self-evident about the origin and use of the simple sod-bricks, I started on a trail of research that led back to Indian life in the Rio Grande Valley before the Spanish conquest. Although terrones are still well known to thousands of Spanish-Americans and Indians there, I found no reference to them in scientific, popular, or architectural writings, except a photo-legend in an old plant ecology textbook which referred erroneously to a terron-stack as "adobes."

Adobes are molded from a soil-water mix, whereas terrones are earth-bricks cut from the surface layer of soil in natural meadows. In terrones the soil is firmly bound together by the roots and horizontal underground stems of salt grass, rushes, and less commonly by yerba-mansa and a few other species. Such bricks are fourteen to sixteen inches long, and six to eight wide. Those cut by sharpened, straight spade are six inches deep, machine-cut ones only four. No effort is made to remove the dead grass tops, for these are nestled down into the mud mortar as the inverted brick is laid up in the wall. The dry weight of the subterranean plant parts in a terron ranges up to 3.8 per cent of that of the soil alone. Their bulk is much greater than that weight figure would suggest, and the fine roots especially are very effective in binding the brick together. A heavy clay with abundant fine roots makes the best terron, but even a coarse sand with as little as fifteen per cent of clay can be consolidated sufficiently by twenty years of plant growth in a terron meadow. The meadows on the flood plain of the Rio Grande are alkaline, often showing a white efflorescence over the soil surface.

Experienced terron cutters say that abundance of roots is more important than the texture of the soil. One of my experiments involved removing all the soil by alternately washing and kneading. After this, the weft of *organic material alone* maintained the original form and sharp edges and corners of the terron brick. The pervasive binding effect of the roots and rhizomes makes it possible to pry these bricks by crowbar from an old wall for use again, whereas adobe brick is completely ruined by such treatment.

I watched Isleta Indian men cutting terrones from meadows which had been so used for generations. Only one of them, Benny Garcia, was making it his full time career. A few Spanish American farmers are part-time cutters, using a crude, heavy wood-plank apparatus pulled behind a truck. Terrones sell for one-third the price of adobes. The oldest occupied dwellings of any kind in the middle Rio Grande valley are the ancient terron homes of Pueblo Indians which are of unknown but venerable age. Also, the mission at Isleta Pueblo, built sometime before 1629 and still in use as a place of worship, is of terron construction with the bricks hidden by plaster.

Many Spanish-Americans in the valley near Albuquerque strongly prefer terrones over adobes because they withstand flood waters, which rapidly dissolve adobe houses. I submerged a thoroughly hardened, good quality adobe brick, weighing 29.5 pounds, in a tub of water. It began disintegrating at once. After two and a half hours, the adobe had fallen apart completely, leaving no solid fragment. In contrast, one Isleta and one Sandia terron were kept submerged for thirty days, following which there was no sign that any soil whatever had been lost. The edges and corners remained as angular as before. Another saltgrass terron, thoroughly saturated after soaking for twelve days, bore a weight of 620 pounds with very slight visible compression that squeezed out only a trace of water. This weight is twice that of the wall upon a brick of the bottom tier. Usually, because of the much better bond obtained, clay mud is used instead of cement mortar in laying up the bricks; in this case the vulnerable point during a prolonged flood is the mortar rather than the terrones.

A visitor to a fur farm is supposed to have asked how often each mink can be skinned. A different answer would apply to terron fields, for they are harvested repeatedly. The more clay and the less sand in the soil, the more frequently may they be cut. Meadows of varying ages since last cut, and one at least thirty years in continuous growth (hence, if ever cut, fully recovered) furnished a good series of square-meter plots, illustrating four stages of plant succession.

Nails driven into a terron wall hold firmly and do not damage the brick. This makes possible a novel method of applying plaster, whereby stucco-netting is not needed. The builder densely studs the wall with roofing-nails, leaving the heads projecting a half-inch; then he may apply a coat of modern stucco. But an even simpler method is practicable. A "plaster" made of clay mud is smeared over the terrones without any support but the grass tops and projecting roots and soil irregularities. The bond is better than it would be with a cement mortar or stucco.

Most owners replaster the outside after three or four years. A good "mud dauber" achieves a most pleasing and appropriate finish with this humble medium. The open network of broad shallow fissures gives the effect of the broad bark-plates of an aged western yellow pine, as though the house, like a tree, had grown up out of the ground. In a sense it has.

Plastering the outside is chiefly to give the house a more finished appearance. In the dry climate of this region (8.5 inches annual precipitation), there is scarcely any weathering of terron walls. Therefore, many terron homes in the country are left unplastered. In those cases, it is possible to tell at a glance, while driving past, whether adobe or terron bricks were used. The high organic content of the latter makes them a much darker brown than adobes. And, by stopping to examine a wall more closely, one sees plant roots and usually grass tops in the inverted terrones.

On seeing their first unplastered terron house, most people are inclined to scorn this inexpensive building material. This is quite unjustified, for no houses are cooler in the hot southwestern summer or easier to heat in winter. While, inch for inch, soil is not as good an insulating material as many others, the much greater thickness of terron or adobe walls insures year-round comfort. I found many large, modern houses finished with stucco that are made of terrones without appearing so. One of these was occupied by a prosperous physician and his family.

During the nineteenth century, terrones were more commonly used in villages and farms of the region than any other building material. In one barn built about 1850, the terrones were twenty-two inches long; they had required two men for lifting them. The walls had withstood the disastrous Rio Grande flood of 1874 which ruined many adobe structures.

Among the early Spanish inhabitants, a young man about to be married had no housing worries. It was customary for him to build a terron house for his bride, using one of the walls of his parents' home as the starting point of the new house. Up to a point, the best terron houses are those built most slowly. Since new terron walls inevitably settle somewhat, the builder allows pauses for this as the walls go up. After each five or six tiers he waits for a few weeks before resuming work. Perhaps this adds to the popularity of terron construction.

Of the many villagers and farmers with whom I talked, all seemed pleased with their lot and at peace with the world. They have not, like so many Anglo couples, mortgaged their distant futures merely for shelter from the elements, a simple natural right of mankind through the ages. For comfort, availability, and economy, the terron, in its proper setting, is a splendid natural building material for people "living close to the soil."

26

THE TROPICS: A PLACE OF TURNING

THE sphere of the heavens was known long before the earthly one, and the two turning points of the sun, at solstice times, were called "tropics." The sun, when it turns back to go the opposite direction, is in the constellation Cancer or Capricorn. Another familiar use of the root word is found in the biological term for a turning—"tropism."

Logically, should not a map of the southern hemisphere or of any place in it be printed and marked with south, not north, at the top of the sheet? That such maps are not so oriented is just one of the indications that the cultures of the north have dominated those of the south in world thought. Yet we of the north are profoundly ignorant of the tropics and the south generally; I have even seen purported world maps that omit New Zealand. Our ideas of the tropics come from Tarzan, travel posters, and "Some Enchanted Evening."

Two imaginary, roughly east-west lines on the planet are significant: the isotherms of a mean annual temperature of 24° C. or 75° F. The tropics of the world, from the standpoint of climate, people, soil, plants and animals, lie in the zone between these lines. There the paramount fact of life is the sun.

Summer noondays in Antarctica, and in most of the rest of the southern hemisphere, the sun's highest position is in the north; in northern lands it climbs to a peak in the south. But in tropical regions the sun is not far from directly overhead at noon. It casts very short shadows during the middle hours of the day, and its rays are hot because they traverse less of the atmosphere's thickness. The days are of moderate length throughout the year—not very long in summer, not very short in winter. This means there is really no winter or summer as most of us know them, though there may be, as in Costa Rica, as many as eight fairly distinct seasons.

Thus, the power of the tropical sun goes hand in hand with the second cardinal point of tropical ecology, the lack of a real winter. The valuable clean-up effect of winter frost—the killing of minute eggs and spores—is missing. The eggs of worms and the cysts of protozoans survive indefinitely; they are stockpiled. It is best not to put your fingers into your mouth, not to eat anything picked up from the floor, not to let the baby play there. The tropics provide a paradise for fungi; their spores are everywhere, and they flourish. Dead wood decays with amazing rapidity. In the rain forests most of the mineral nutrients are tied up in the living mass of vegetation, so that one walks over the forest floor without scuffing up dead leaves or branches. In the soil, organic matter and essential minerals are very deficient. Nature allows man to raise crops successfully only about two years in the traditional slash and burn system of agriculture. The subsistence farmer must then cut down another piece of forest to make a new, equally short-lived field. With burgeoning population, tropical "third-world" countries fall further and further behind in the capacity to feed themselves. How long will the humus in our own soils withstand the drain of our attempting to feed the world?

The absence of winter and the typical high rainfall and humidity encourage tropical green plants to be rather constantly active. Plants having different light requirements occupy all levels from the soil to the top of the tree canopy. Epiphytes (upon plants) are far more conspicuous than in northern hemisphere forests. They make their own food from light, water, and carbon dioxide like other green plants, hence epiphytes are not parasites. The epiphytic plants represent various taxonomic groups, through algae, liverworts and mosses to the flowering plants. The latter group of epiphytes includes chiefly some members of the orchid and pineapple families. Large and very common "tank epiphytes" of the pineapple (bromeliad) group can hold around their leaf-bases as much as five gallons of rain-water per plant. Taken collectively, these plants constitute the fascinating "aerial swamp" which harbors examples of all the major groups of non-marine animals. Dry areas are also found in places in the tropics, but the world's principal deserts lie a bit farther north and south.

There is no season when insects are not prevalent, but people are not driven mad by them as sometimes happens in the arctic and subarctic. In many towns and cities, not even window screens are needed. Breeding seasons of birds tend to be mixed up. Mammals show little or no activity in preparing for a coming season. They do not hibernate, and are scarcely adapted in either structural or behavioral ways for changes of season.

We in the temperate zone are accustomed to a wide range of temperature during the year. But the range in any one day is limited, usually amounting to less than thirty degrees Fahrenheit. In the tropics one finds just the opposite; the big change is not annual but diurnal, so that one often needs a coat after sunset. Without frost, there is a dearth of physical weathering to influence the formation of soil. Therefore, soil is produced largely through chemical changes.

In short, physical factors operate differently in the tropical environment, and the challenges to life are consequently different. And so are the ways by which living things meet them for survival and reproduction. Since most biologists are trained in temperate regions, they find endless fascination in the teeming, steaming, stinking, threatening, lovely life of the tropics.

27

IT CAN'T HAPPEN HERE

A durable people who lived, and whose descendents still live, in tropical America are the Mayan Indians. Their culture surpassed by orders of magnitude that of the Ancient Ones who dwelt in such eyries as Mesa Verde, Betatakin, and Keet Seel in our own Southwest. Although certainly different, it was comparable in level, and in a few ways even superior, to the European civilization contemporaneous with it.

Its most astonishing aspect is the sheer volume of the aggregate Mayan construction in the limestone country of Yucatan, Nicaragua, and Guatemala. Only the smallest fraction of their temples, markets, courts, athletic fields, plazas, and limestone sinkhole cenotes have yet been excavated. Supplied by Nature with a bedrock ideally suited for massive edifices, the Mayans long maintained a stable culture in the unstable tropics. No one knows for certain what brought down this culture. If we are to enter the low valuation they placed on human life as a score against them, it is well to remember that the early Celtic May Day was also associated with human sacrifice.

Each of the major areas of excavated ruins which we saw there exhibits its own distinctive character. What is impressive at renowned Chichen Itza is its mix of scope, variety, the romance of the sacrificial pool in the deep cenote, and the modern touch of overemphasis on organized sport. It was surely an incentive for ball players to excel when a team would lose their heads along with the game.

Not to have seen the splendid decorative sculpture on the walls of the varied buildings at Uxmal would be a loss. At

Sayil only one major temple has been cleared from the centuries accumulation of overgrowing dry forest, but near its top one may touch a crucial supporting beam that gives a more forceful impression of antiquity than any rock, for wood has lived. Cross the road from the great ruin at Kabah, and follow a trail a quarter-mile to a splendid arch that marks the south end of an ancient paved road which has a similar arch at its north end twenty miles distant.

In visiting all the ruins to be seen on a six-hundred mile circuit drive, we saw no minor ruin, even, which we wished we had not bothered to reach. Thoreau inveighed against ruins of "hammered stone," claiming to prefer the stone fence around an honest man's field, but Thoreau never saw the Mayan country.

The high point of our ruin-rummaging was, literally and figuratively, Palenque; it lies somewhat off the beaten track and entertains fewer visitors than others. Mountainous, heavily forested scenery sets off the ancient temples to perfection. The excavated structures, instead of towering above scrubby dry-forest cover, are overtopped by trees of a Tropical Moist Forest. As we walked up the steep approach road in the early morning, with remnant night mists rising among the buttressed, crowded trunks, the finest group of temples burst into view against the forest backdrop, the ground between them carpeted with brilliant green meadow.

Among the many distinctions of the Palenque buildings is the relative abundance of original color on old plastered walls, at places in the Palace where it is protected from sunlight. Loss of the bright colors across the centuries seems to be the most striking difference between what we see today and how its creators saw their handiwork.

The best part of the Palenque experience is in the Temple of the Inscriptions, descending alone and silent as each of us managed it, down the sixty-six steep, cool, dimly-lit stone steps to the famous tomb deep inside the base. I calculated that each cautious step downward was taking me about a score of years backward in time. One has reached the year 692 A.D. when he arrives at the lowest level, where the ruler Pakal once rested amid precious ornaments and offerings and guarded by nine priestly statues larger than life.

The original five-ton lid of the ten-by-seven-foot sarcophagus is seen dimly illuminated, as it must have been while the pyramid was being erected around and above it so that it could never be removed. This massive rock lid is completely covered on the upper surface by symbolic bas-relief carving, the subject of a notorious recent controversy. The figure of Pakal was claimed to depict an ancient astronaut, with his body reclined and his hands on the controls of a space-ship from a still older, more remote civilization. However, the Mayan sculptors were closer to Nature than to technological surprises, and the authorities on their lives recognize a stylized *Ceiba* tree and its flowers and fruit, with other symbolic natural things such as the sculptors and Pakal knew on this their native planet.

At another region of Mayan ruins we saw the god Chacmool, not as a face with an upward-hooked nose as commonly seen in temple friezes, but depicted full figure as a settee, lying on his back with knees drawn up at one end and his head and shoulders lifted at the other, leaving a place where one could sit in between. The only other visitor, a young, full-blooded Mayan man, joined me silently at this shrine of his ancestors. Finally raising his eyes to mine for the first time, he reverently murmered "Chac-mool!" Feeling that these were the only words we understood in common, I nodded, repeating "Chac-mool."

I, and perhaps he too, saw a symbolic difference in our racial histories. His descent was from a hot-climate culture in which people had worshiped a settee, an image of relaxation and stability. My ancestors, in lands that changed from tropical in summer to polar each winter, had developed a very different sort of civilization through worship of the Wheel, a concept that the Mayans thought worthy only of children's toys. It is the symbol not of stability but its obverse—perpetual change.

Only time, which the Mayan scientists and priests studied with great care, can tell whether our accelerating motion and change represent true progress and the permanence which eluded that strange Indian culture in the even stranger tropics.

28

AN AMERICAN INVASION OF EASTER ISLAND

THE venerable windjammer *Bear* took a different and slower course across the Pacific, stopping at Tahiti. But we aboard Admiral Byrd's expedition flagship *Pacific Fir* were drawn to the "Navel of the World" by magnetized imaginations, as the lodestone base of Easter Island has deflected mariner's compasses throughout recorded history. Easter or Rapanui has long stood as a symbol of the ancient human mysteries. This land has seen much of the horror of men killing and eating men. It was long tyrranized by the worship of the dead, the priestly Long-ears immortalized in the somber statuary. Later, a birdman cult started a tradition for celebrating new life, the divine life in the egg of the Sooty Tern. The ceremony included races through shark-infested waters by swimmers intent on bringing back, from the jagged nesting rocks offshore, the first egg of each new breeding season.

We more modern Byrdmen sensed an aura of utter strangeness in the dark burial *ahu* and the vacant-eyed statues leaning awry in brooding silence on Rano-raraku's seaward slope. That it was the modern world of 1933 meant nothing to the polyglot natives—they seemed to be adrift and lost in Time. Easter was so far from the shipping lanes that only one vessel visited it, a ship of the Chilean navy that came and went once annually to bring the natives simple supplies, and take off sheep products and usually the relieved governor. We saw no sign of any industry among the mixed Polynesian-Melanesian natives except the carving and trading of small images of wood or stone, and spear-fishing in the surf.

No other nation has accused Chile of imperialism over this island which lacks natural resources. Measuring fifteen miles east-west and ten north-south, it consists of several coalesced volcanic peaks. Though well isolated, it is considered the easternmost island of Polynesia. On dropping anchor near the sole occupied village, Hanga Roa, we were honored by a state visit by the cordial governor, an officer of his country's navy who cheerfully explained that, on conviction of embezzling government funds, he was being punished by this appointment for one year.

Three shipmates and I, hoping to get to Image Mountain at the far end of the island, borrowed horses and obtained a guide. This native, carrying our haversacks with our food and equipment on his horse, pressed on out of sight while we were collecting plants and lizards. We saw him no more. He had stolen my binoculars, and from Paul Siple a better pair of binocs and a brand-new Leica camera. Paul later replaced his loss by purchases in New Zealand.

Because the trail faded away and loose volcanic bombs roughened the ground too much for horses, we tied up the animals to await the return trip. On parts of the pumice plain having little plant cover, we were delighted to find several antique spear-heads (*matai*) of black volcanic glass, probably relics of the desperate fighting in the 1600s when the commoners threw off the yoke of the priesthood and overthrew the statues they had been forced to fashion. The weapons were different from conventional spears in not being pointed; the black obsidian had been shaped into a crescent with a sharp, glassy cutting edge. The spear was swung across throat or abdomen instead of being thrown or thrusted.

An obscure opening in rough "aa" lava tempted our sailor friend to squirm into it. He felt around in near darkness and touched a mouldering human skull. At his signal, we pulled him out by the feet, and saw that he had some other human bones also. After photographing these remains, we should have replaced them, but our group failed this test of sensitivity. The natives had their ways of being amoral, and we had ours.

On the south or seaward flank of Rano-raraku, we examined and photographed the gigantic stone images of the Long-ears. We did not, fortunately, try to solve any of the well-publicized mysteries of Easter Island. The upper ends of the statues projected from the ground, pointing helter-skelter in different directions. On the steeper slope, soil-slippage had buried some up to the rope-like ears. A few were toppled over completely, and one large image was lying supine. These tight-lipped messengers from a forgotten age evoked the same awe that one feels in a grove of giant sequoias.

High up on this volcanic slope one may climb into the breached crater, where the statues had been painfully chipped out of the tuff rock inside the circular rim. Some still lay there in various stages of completion, still attached to the parent rock and staring up to the sky from eyeless sockets. It is believed that the gargantuan project was suddenly interrupted by a rebellion of the plebes. We saw rough, heavy stone adzes (*toki*) of basalt lying about among the unfinished images, where it is said the workmen threw them down on the last day of work. To us amateurs, though, they appeared to be badly enough worn or broken to have been discarded as useless while the work was still going on.

The evening was darkening, the wind rising as though a storm was coming, and the trail back to the village at the other end of the island was long and hard. After hours of plodding and riding, we saw the ocean beyond the north side of the island. It was a surprise to see the *Fir*, which we had left anchored just off the village, now far out to sea and apparently moving. Was it leaving us ashore until its return from Antarctica nearly two years later?

Long after dark, footsore and exhausted and cold, we spotted a bonfire gleaming on the beach near the dock. On finally reaching it, we found a few shipmates who had also missed the boat; they clustered around a black, missionary-style cooking pot which hung over the fire. We learned that our ship had put to sea in order to ride out a storm expected that night. Thus, we were marooned without food of our own, adequate clothing, or blankets and camping gear.

The charitable element in the village population had come forward and were contributing food items to a Macbeth-type witches brew in the huge pot. It contained pheasant and chicken scraps, intact eggs of both fowl, probably lizard meat, and possibly other comestibles best not inquired into. It tasted wonderful!

A small native appeared from the windy darkness and wordlessly loaned to me a ragged blue suit-coat with brass buttons and decorative braid. It had once belonged to a naval officer much smaller than I, but it was most welcome, for night air is cool in the tropics. The natives indicated by sign language that we could sleep, one man to each of their surf-boats stored in shelters with thatched roofs supported by poles at the corners and with all sides open. We slept, or tried to, in what clothes we had, without other covering or padding, getting some protection from the sea wind by the boat's sides, and supported at infrequent intervals along our bodies by the narrow wooden ribs running across the boat's curved bottom. As a sleeping arrangement, this impressed us deeply.

Before the *Fir* dropped anchor nearby the next morning, Siple and I patrolled the rocky shore at low tide, collecting the largely unfamiliar invertebrates while carefully avoiding the tentacles of stranded Portuguese Men of War. Soon after we boarded the ship, Easter Island was disappearing below the horizon beyond the stern.

The clockwork of the starry sky gains new and unpredictable dimensions of movement from the rolling and pitching of a ship at sea. Those who really see the night sky are fortunate, for as an astronomer friend points out, light-pollution from cities and towns destroys it. As viewed far from population centers, our glimpse into the cosmos, shallow at best, must be the ultimate of non-living beauty both visually and conceptually. Thought and feeling are stirred anew each clear night in coming to terms with the firmament, for beyond the relatively little actually seen is a deep regress into our history, mythology, and psychology.

Judging from the fact that men persist in banishing the night artificially whenever and wherever possible, it seems that, despite our spoken fears of many threats about which we take no action from year to year, what must really bother us most is the outdoor night with its loneliness and testament to our insignificance. This is seldom what people mean by being "close to Nature," but it may be the basic essence of that. This species of fear, like the related "fear of God," is not terrifying, not depressing, but exhilarating.

Through the ages, people have done such coming to terms most intimately from a base in deserts or on ocean waters. At sea, though, there is always invisible or visible moisture in the air to dull the stars, and the most remote desert is overspread with wind-driven dusts and pollens. On the surface of this planet, one can get closest to the stars at our own destination, through the pure winter skies of Antarctica.

Homeward bound in 1935 after our far southern exposure, we dropped anchor again off Hanga Roa, to trade for more of the native carvings. I was called above deck with the unlikely story that the new governor of Easter Island wanted to see me. With a grin, he handed over my binoculars, slightly damaged but usable. Then he recounted with relish how he had recently seen at a distance a native using my stolen glasses. Later the man denied knowing anything about them, so the governor ordered him trussed up and left lying out on the ground until he saw fit to confess. After an uncomfortable night, the thief led the gendarmerie to the hiding place. The other binocs and the Leica remained lost; the latter was probably thrown into the sea when the native realized he could not use it in the absence of film or processing.

The dusky men who boarded ship with the governor brought many "heemages" for trading. Although Easter is nearly treeless, the wooden images were carved from leguminous trees found there. These trade items, from one to five feet tall, were stylized depictions of an emaciated god seen in a vision by an ancient holy man. The chest was deeply scored to suggest ribs seen through starved skin. The chief resemblance to the famed stone statues is in the long ears. I cherish more the genuine antique needles (*eavy*) which I obtained for several "long-time shirtees," a high price. The needles were made by their ancestors from bones of the sea birds that laid the desperately-sought eggs of the birdman ritual. The natives wanted wearing apparel but never shoes. The skin on the soles of their feet seemed to be half an inch thick, enabling them to walk even over sharp lava. Cakes of soap failed to interest them.

When we visited Easter Island, its principal interest and charm was that its present was essentially identical with its past. Presumably, that is what many tourists are looking for when they visit cultures different than their own, but the more of them do so, the less diversity they are able to find. Even fifty years ago, substantial identity with the past could be claimed for few places on earth, and Easter Island was in their forefront.

Entrepreneurs have brought progress to Easter Island. Transients are welcomed for their money; seeing white faces is no longer a novelty. There is now an airstrip and a luxury hotel. The antiquity tends to be obscured by a layer of hokum. Leis, luas, and hulas are not native to Easter Island, and it is not intrinsically a cheerful place. Intrinsically, it is an interesting place.

The modern dilemma, similar to that of our wilderness areas with increasing visitation, is accompanied by human compensations, however. More visitors are able to enjoy this still interesting place, without having to sleep across the ribs of surf-boats. In the Thirties, the natives did not seem happy, and by our standards they were far from prosperous. We hope that their lot has improved in both respects, judged by their own standards.

29

THE ICEBERG GRAVEYARD AND
ART GALLERY

ADMIRAL Byrd, who had an undeniable dramatic flair, posted a memo on the bulletin board in the 'tween-decks area of the *Pacific Fir*. It warned that we had all been living in a fool's paradise, cruising through foggy, ice-filled seas too fast and without proper precautions for coping with icebergs and growlers. True, we had already filled in the ship's forepeak from bottom to top of the hull with concrete. But now an iceberg watch was to be posted on the bow, and the bridge and engine room would be on constant alert to change direction and speed.

The old *Bear*, our historic oaken icebreaker from the Alaska Service, would have been the far safer vessel for these conditions, but she was still under sail from Tahiti to New Zealand. We in the flagship *Fir* had cruised southeast from Dunedin and were now in quite unknown waters, hundreds of miles from any possible source of rescue in case of disaster. "We were the first that ever burst/Into that silent sea."

December 16, 1933. The Exec [Commander George Noville] came around this morning with his jovial leer to assign me, although he is unaware of my abnormal farsightedness, to iceberg watches from 2:00 to 4:00 AM and PM until further notice. This job started today. A heavier swell than usual was running, and a following wind made it so chilly that I needed a sheepskin coat and gloves. Soon after taking a stand on the forepeak, I saw something very large swimming out of the thick fog ahead, or so it seemed.

It appeared to be differentiated into an eerie head and a swirling, eel-like body. It came head-first past our port side and disappeared into the fog aft. Saw no icebergs, but several more "sea serpents" at closer range appeared to be huge brown algae, some branched and others with a few large, bur-like fruiting bodies. I stood watch fifty minutes beyond my two-hour stint, since the fog ahead was so thick that it would not have been safe to leave and track down my successor. Saw Wilson's Storm Petrels and at least fifty White-faced Storm Petrels. I had not noticed before that it stays really light all night.

When I awakened next morning, the old freighter was kicking up her heels in a furious gale, force 70, with the first snowfall of the expedition. The Condor plane with its 84-foot wingspread was still lashed to the after deck, but had just sustained a broken aileron, and we had to secure her better. Seas from starboard swept the deck, carrying several men with them but not overboard. Because of some problem in the engine room, the ship wallowed in the wave-troughs for an hour before we could get her turned head on, to avoid further damage to our principal exploratory plane. Since the ship's bow was plunging into green water, my lookout for bergs had to be from the bridge. During this watch I saw my first Light-mantled Sooty Albatross, a smaller bird than the legendary Wandering Albatross with its eleven-foot wing reach.

Our first iceberg, the dim outline of a tall cathedral spire rearing above the horizon, appeared on December 19. Soon I was busy at the forepeak, signaling the helmsman the position of inconspicuous but dangerous, low-riding growlers of solid, green-blue ice derived from the break-up of old bergs. The ship would weave in and out among them at half-speed. During my afternoon watch we passed hundreds of large bergs, and oceanic birds were becoming abundant—more Albatrosses, Silver-gray Petrels, and a few Giant Fulmar. The white, dove-like Snow Petrels swung out of the mists like wraiths, and back in again. The Admiral remarked that he had seen more icebergs during this one day than on the whole of his previous antarctic expedition.

The next day, when we crossed the Antarctic Circle, I saw from my watch in the crow's nest the first leopard seal, that great swift predator feared by man, beast, and bird. Only the killer whale is the greater hazard to men on a floating ice pan in the southern pack ice. Soon we noted sea leopards pursuing young crab-eater seals on the low sea ice. Crab-eaters can move as fast as a man can run over hard-packed snow.

The summer solstice on December 21 found us in a peculiar situation, for at 66° 31′ S. by 149° 49′ W. we had sailed beyond the sunset on the very day the sun began its northward sojourn. On this midsummer day of perfect weather, we found a broad, open patch of ocean and prepared for Byrd's exploratory flight toward the unknown continental coast. I was assigned to calculate and assemble emergency rations and gear to use in case the Condor was forced down. This first flight of the expedition was one the Admiral later termed the most important of his life, though he had navigated the first planes to fly to the North Pole, South Pole, and another on a pioneer Atlantic crossing. The observations and aerial photography erased much putative continental land from the world map and demonstrated continuity there between the Ross Sea and the Pacific. While the waiting *Fir* was hove-to, Senior-Scientist Poulter and I shot some graceful sea-birds which I made up for the museum. When it snowed a few days later, the ship's mate, a New Zealander, soberly affirmed that the cause of the storm was our shooting of Snow Petrels. This was not the only time the ancient Albatross syndrome came to light in our sailors' conversation.

Christmas Day was to be very special for more than the significance of the day and the excellence of the dinner. Following the latter I went on iceberg watch as usual. Because the fog was extremely dense, the vessel should have stopped altogether, but Admiral Byrd, looking like a Tyrone Power in a fur parka, came forward to tell me that we were so far behind schedule that we had to push on at half speed, and I should keep an especially sharp lookout.

December 25, 1933. Today our world is bounded by a narrow circle of tossing sea which melts into a curtain of impenetrable fog. The eyes of the iceberg man are the eyes of the ship itself; he must be constantly alert for a cliff of ice suddenly leaping at us from the fog. Even at half-speed it would be difficult or impossible to stop or change course in time, especially since bergs often shelve out close beneath the ocean surface.

About an hour after I went off watch, Commodore Gjertsen in the wheelhouse, having absolutely no evidence of a berg ahead, on a sudden inexplicable impulse ordered the vessel halted. She had already slowed considerably when a big berg loomed up dead ahead, and the man on the bow signaled frantically. By spinning the wheel hard over, the helmsman was just able to avoid ramming the colossal berg.

The Commodore had behind him a long career of ice navigation in Arctic waters, but he said that this was the narrowest escape he ever had. To me this day was both Christmas and Thanksgiving.

Two days later we cruised through the white herds all day and night. The bergs were smaller, all old and more or less disintegrating. Old icebergs must be like old elephants, gathering in a particular hallowed spot to await the end. While on bridge lookout I saw one berg quite close to the *Fir* turn over bottoms-up, with a flood of cascading water and avalanches of rotten white ice falling into the seething sea. We were fortunate not to have been any closer, let alone diving *inside* its crystalline caverns as Cousteau's men were to do with courage and rashness in a similar antarctic monster years later. The largest berg seen on this day had massively lobed edges at the water-line, with very deep caves penetrating into its royal-blue mass.

The next day, in an area of bergs even closer to final dissolution, Nature revealed herself as an unimaginably versatile and talented sculptor. We steamed close among decaying bergs that far surpassed any high-piled cumulus clouds for displays of countless varied figures. All that remained of one above the ocean was a white natural bridge the equal of Rainbow Bridge, Utah, in height, sweep, and grandeur. "Dr. Perkins reported today a berg that looked like the face of George Washington according to Gilbert Stuart, and after passing it to see its other side, we saw the bust and head of a colossal young woman as perfect as any human sculptor could have carved on Mount Rushmore or Stone Mountain." We were thus the only ship's crew to actually see her to whom an earlier poet made obeisance as

The white immaculate Virgin of the south
Whose icy hand no mortal ever touched
Whose icy glance no mortal ever dared.

Wondering if this apparition were imagined or near reality, I asked about it among those lucky enough to be on deck at the time, before they had time to compare notes among themselves. This fully confirmed my original informant in his amazing account. The frigid lady was also attested to by the hard-bitten Captain Verleger, who had seen her from the wheelhouse, and quite independently. Perhaps, when such a myriad of disintegrating bergs are seen, the probability of one of them representing a given object of artless art becomes statistically respectable. In number we expect variety—there is thought to be some chance of intelligent life somewhere else in the cosmos, mainly because we see so very many suns which conceivably might have planets like ours, though none of our sun's other planets qualify, and no other star's planets are detectable.

Sleep became a waste of opportunity. Dr. Poulter estimated that during the twenty-four hours of the 28th he saw more than 8,000 full-fledged icebergs in this "Devil's Graveyard" area of the southern sea. Our having blundered among them in a tramp freighter with an ordinary hull having iron plates only 7/8 inch thick could be one of the reasons why British polar authority Brian Roberts wrote of Byrd's two private southern expeditions, "It is impossible not to wonder at the extraordinary risks which were constantly taken without fatal consequences." To us the crowded bergs that left open water among them seemed safer than the heavy pack in the Ross Sea that battered the plates above the engine room. Shearing off a couple of rivet-heads would have been enough to finish us off.

The notorious "Byrd luck" held as well in the almost unprecedented openness of the band of pack ice in that sector at the time we voyaged there. The deepest southward penetration there previously had been Captain James Cook's when, just one hundred and fifty years and one month before us, he reached 71° S. Lat. His ship and ours had probed the sea there at the right time and place, but he had no aircraft for penetrating farther south. In a sea-air combination and in unknown skies, Byrd erased land from the map in a series of well-planned flights. Then we turned about and held the *Fir* westward for Little America.

ANTARCTIC EXPLORER SIPLE

30

THE NATIVITY OF THE WIND CHILL FACTOR

IT is the four-month night of the 1934 winter on the last continent. Weather conditions are too severe at Little America for dog-teams to be worked. After thorough preparation, two young scientists and two trail men leave for a week of observations along the sea-ice edge where the Bay of Whales meets the open Ross Sea. This is only the second winter-night journey in the history of Antarctica. The first, twenty-two years before and four hundred miles farther east, was a biological trip to see breeding Emperor Penguins for the first time. That became known as "the worst journey in the world" from the two volumes with that title by Cherry-Garrard.

The aims of the 1934 trip are locating the winter position of the seacoast in or beyond the Bay mouth and observing seals there, if any; collecting clean snow for bacteriological analyses; and shaking down his group for a sledging exploration of unknown eastern land the next summer. The leader is Paul Siple, who heads the expeditions's biology department. Six years before, the 19-year-old Paul had won the nationwide competition by which the Boy Scout movement selected an Eagle Scout to represent Scouting on the first Byrd Antarctic Expedition.

Man-hauling heavy sledges over irregular pressure-ice is brutal work even at reasonable temperatures. This party encounters twenty-mile wind at temperatures of minus 50° F. and colder. The geologist had forgotten to bring his protective mask, so wraps many thicknesses of a heavy woolen scarf about his face. This proves inadequate; his face is severely frost-bitten and after three days they return to us, pulling him on a sledge.

Dr. Potaka, our half-Maori physician, treats the swollen face, which eventually will return to normal. Paul asks the doctor just how wind and cold work in combination, and is told that no one understands either the physics or the physiology of it. Paul's comment is, "Then someone should certainly find out."

The man who did so, several years later, was Dr. Paul Siple. The shock of his friend's hazard had set him wondering and thinking.

In his doctorate thesis, on the effect of polar climates on explorers, Siple included only general, qualitative material. He sent the manuscript to me for critical comments. If I had suggested that he gather hard, cold data, then systematize and tabulate the effects on humans, I would have become the godfather of the wind chill factor. But I didn't have the mind to. Paul thought of these things himself, not in time for his thesis, but in time to carry out, with Charles Passel, the necessary experiments outdoors at Little America III on his return in 1940.

Paul Allman Siple spent more years on the white continent than anyone else. His career bridges the historic crevasse between the heroic age of "iron men and wooden ships" and the present dominance of Big Science, when few need to winter over and an adventure is when something goes wrong in the routine. For twelve continuous months he lived at the precise South Pole, directing the scientific work during and after the International Geophysical Year, 1957-58. Often he felt upon his face the wind of the farthest south at its most chill.

Even today, what I prefer to call the "Siple Factor" is more familiar in the hearing than in the understanding. The technical paper was published in 1945, but the wind chill concept had not caught on with the general public until about the time of Paul's untimely death in 1968.

Nearly everyone knows that bodily comfort does not depend on just one atmospheric factor at a given time. We say, "It isn't the heat, it's the humidity." But of course it's both, in combination. In very dry air at a certain temperature, comfort is equal to what it would be in humid air that is 16° cooler. Green plants are at the mercy of "vapor pressure deficit" or the drying pull of air, which is also the resultant of forces working in concert.

During Paul's third stay overwinter at Little America, when he commanded that base for the U. S. Antarctic Service, he and his associate tested the freezing power of moving air compared with calm air. Water, rather than mercury or alcohol, was used as the cooling body in their experiments because of its physiological significance. The 1945 paper clarified and standardized empirical knowledge on the cooling effect of wind, or how temperature and wind combine to affect the comfort-safety level.

Two ways of expressing the relationship are useful. The simpler one is the familiar table of figures which renders the combined effect in figures *equivalent* to the effect of cold alone in a dead calm. Most laymen find it convenient to think in these terms. The figures in the body of the chart are not actual temperatures, but express solely in temperature terms the effect on human flesh of a given combination of temperature and wind. That is, they are *equivalent* temperatures in degrees Fahrenheit.

The same investigators also developed an actual index to wind chill, expressed in the formula

$$K_0 = (v \times 100 + 10.15 - v)(33 - T_a)$$

where v is wind velocity in meters per second, T_a is air temperature in degrees C., and K_0 is wind chill in kilocalories per square meter per hour. (Find meters per second by multiplying miles per hour by 0.447).

Conditions for outdoor travel are no longer pleasant at indices higher than 1200 on sunny days and 1000 on foggy and overcast days. Freezing of exposed human flesh should be expected at a value of about 1400. Siple's 1934 winter party to the Ross Sea, when one man suffered bad frostbite, endured a 2455 index.

The antarctic story from 1940 until Siple's passing at age 59 was to a large extent his biography. He also served the nation during World War II as an inventor-climatologist. Americans in jungles, deserts, and the Arctic benefited in comfort and even survival from his military atlas of clothing and climate, in which he worked out, from field and laboratory testing, the clothing assemblages needed for each month in the various operation areas. With a colleague, he conceived and developed the famous thermal-barrier (or vapor barrier) boot. He perfected the cold-weather parka to its present efficiency. A mountain and an island bear his name, and the New Zealand government named the Siple Coast. As a statesman of science he promoted the Antarctic Treaty of 1959 which made the continent an international, demilitarized and uncommercialized park for scientific research, and he served as scientific attache to our embassy in Australia. In his home lab, he developed ideas resulting in several patents, and as a hobby he studied the behavior of the spin axis of spheres revolving freely in air-jets, simulating the planet and its wobble.

Throughout his geographical discoveries, theoretical studies, practical inventions, and administrative problems, Paul retained the eager curiosity of the youthful Scout—imaginative, original, flexible in mind, never frozen into academic or professional postures. Lacking the grim single-mindedness conveyed in portraits of early explorers, he gave one the impression that whatever he did was mainly for fun. If he feared anything in Antarctica, it was falling into a crevasse of career specialization. Siple was the versatile generalist whose work made a continent (almost) safe for specialists.

Those who go to Antarctica today either pay for it (tourists) or are paid for it (employees). Those motivations seem, to the Byrd volunteers whose shipmates were science and adventure, quite different from "the first fine careless rapture" which lured them southward. Little America itself, bearing the poignancy of a legendary Brigadoon or Germelshausen, softens focus into a scene in time but not in space. Last seen embedded in an iceberg in 1963, 200 miles out in the Ross Sea, perhaps it is still drifting in those remote waters where the dying icebergs congregate.

Along the coast of the frozen land which Paul first explored on the great sledging expedition he led in his youth, Mount Siple gleams in the midnight sun ten thousand feet over pack ice and shelf ice. It commemorates one of the immortals of polar exploration.

31

MY ISLANDS

THREE years went by after my islands were named before I discovered them myself. No physical rigors or intrepid shipmates were involved; in fact, I accomplished it in my easy chair at home. It happened while I was perusing the coastline on a big folding map someone had loaned me, which was then the most recent map of the entire continent of Antarctica and the seas around it.

Evidently I examined it with some care, for I noted in small type, very close to the mainland along the western coast, the name "Lindsey Islands." My curiosity was aroused because that is my name too.

In a letter sent to the publisher, I stated that it had puzzled me to find the name for new islands on their map, with no islands shown to go along with it. Were there really such islands near there? If so, exactly where are they, and how did they get that name, in case they knew that?

The brief letter that eventually came in reply indicated that such islands indeed existed. The writer added, with ill-concealed glee, that they had been engraved on the plate originally. However, one of the workmen, in a final check of their product before using the engraving for printing the map, had happened to wipe the whole archipelago of fifteen islands off the plate under the impression that they were flecks of dirt or fly specks. The signer felt that the unmapped islands must be somewhere in the vicinity of the elongated double name that survived for the printed map insert. That settled the matter. The organization was restraining itself without apparent difficulty from any sympathetic or apologetic bowing and scraping over the incident.

Still I wondered how the islands had acquired that particular name. This time I wrote to the official group in the Department of the Interior which has to approve all names proposed in the United States before a place can carry that name. Promptly the Board of Geographic names replied with a letter characterized by sobriety and dignity, as befits constituted authority.

This letter is in reply to your inquiry about the Lindsey Islands. As you may have surmised, the islands off the coast of Antarctica at 73° 35′ S., 102° 24′ W. are named for you.

The salient features of the area were first sighted in 1940 by members of the United States Antarctic Service, led by Rear Admiral Richard E. Byrd. Additional data, permitting delineation of these islands and features along the Walgreen Coast and Eights Coast, were obtained in U. S. Navy Operation Highjump, 1946-47, and the cruise of the USS *Glacier* in

1960, during which the coast was photographed from the air.

In 1960, the Board's Advisory Committee on Antarctic Names recommended nomenclature for use on Navy chart H. O. 6633, then being published to reflect the results of recent exploration. In so doing, the Committee selected several names from personnel on Byrd's antarctic expeditions of 1928-30 and 1933-35. The name Lindsey Islands was approved by the Board in 1960 and included in the decision list printed as a Supplement to the November 1960 *Bulletin* of the U. S. Antarctic Projects Officer, a copy of which is enclosed. When the Board publishes a revised and enlarged gazetteer for Antarctica, a textual description of these islands will be included, citing the facts of discovery and naming given here.

Aldo Leopold posed the question in his *Sand County Almanac*, "Does my share of Alaska mean less to me because I shall never go there?" Since my islands are remote and guarded by grinding pack ice, probably no one will ever land there, at least by boat. But I ask, "Does that make them any less valuable?" Well, yes, I'm afraid that it does, and have no immediate plans to subdivide the property. Come to think of it, I cannot even produce a title document. Even so, after I mentioned the islands in a lecture, a whimsical real estate lady asked me if she could list them.

Don't get me wrong, though. For all the kidding taken and given over these small islands, I still like having islands that will remain my own after I have gone. I am especially pleased that they are the most inaccessible islands on earth, so that in a worst-case scenario they may even become the last islands on the planet where life can continue to pasture freely.

32

THE DOG-TEAM AS WOLF PACK

THE Eskimo dog and the German police dog seem closer to the wolf, both physically and temperamentally, than the other breeds are to that ancestor. The name "husky" dog for the Eskimo breed arose in a curious fashion. White men in the north country early used the nick-name "Huskies" for the Eskimo people. Terming the sledge dog "husky" did not refer to the animal's size, strength, or endurance. It simply meant that the dog belonged to an Eskimo. A husky dog is the dog of a Husky.

Husky dogs show every evidence of loving their work, straining at harness and yelping to get going. Once released for the trail, the team takes off explosively. The word "mush" may be used as a starting signal elsewhere than in the pages of Jack London and Robert W. Service, but the only verbal starter I have heard used is "Yake!" It cuts through a brisk wind or snowstorm more incisively than "Mush!" As in driving horses, "gee" directs a right turn, "haw" a left.

Sledge dogs fight frequently among themselves when able to get at each other. The small, black and white, Siberian sledge dogs are particularly savage against dog opponents; other breeds of sledge dogs seldom push a fight to the death. I have never known Siberians or other huskies to snarl at or attack a man, and the bond between dogs and their driver is a beautiful thing to see and experience. Dogs are now obsolescent for polar expeditions, but no modern explorer can feel the same affection for his mechanical Weasel on trail trips.

A wide-ranging vocabulary of expletives is considered an essential qualification for a dog-driver. Much of his work is preventing and breaking up fights and untangling the snarl of harness and dogs. Despite the apparent free-for-all into which he must leap, a driver is not bitten except by sheer accident. Few drivers are ethologists, but a theoretical and practical understanding of canid social relations, including those between dogs and their driver, should be useful. Social relationships have been thoroughly studied in packs of wild wolves, and dogs are not long removed from these ancestors.

The unbounded affection between a dog and driver can be expressed in the unemotional parlance of the animal behaviorist. He realizes that dog social relations derive from the ancestral wolf pack. A human driver becomes a member of the dog pack and its dominant member, being accepted as its leader whether he operates from the rear, as he usually does, or from in front. It need not surprise us that animals may interpret a man as a part of their social group, since in early "imprinting" the human is accepted even as a parent. When a "domesticated" wolf seizes a person's wrist to enforce submission, without crunching down with its powerful jaws, the wise human does not pull away or resist. Sledge dogs do not challenge the dominance of their driver in any such overt fashion. They fight among themselves for social rank, and in some circumstances over food. The frequency of fights indicates that dominance relationships are not clearly established and rigidly maintained as in wolves. Normal social relationships among the huskies are frustrated, probably by man's dominance. The driver enforces or tries to enforce a truce among the team members, but it is an uneasy truce. He prevents the team from settling the rank order for itself in the way a wolf pack determines clear dominance-submission patterns. Except within the pairs in a standard seven-dog team, individual dogs are kept apart as much as possible. The center line maintains a substantial distance between pairs when the dogs are pulling.

After a day of travel, each dog is unfastened from the central line, and snapped on to a fixed point along a staked-out cable, out of reach of neighboring dogs. In winter, we kept each dog chained to the front end of its individual crate which alternated with other boxes along the two sides of man-size tunnels completely buried under the snow. All this human control frustrates the working out of their inherited psychology, whereas the wolf-pack functions smoothly, through a well-understood organization that promotes survival in the wild.

During the darkest and coldest part of the four-month winter night at Little America, the dog Toby broke his chain, found his way out of the sub-snow tunnel system, and left camp. We gave Toby up for lost, for no food could be found out on the high barrier ice, and no shelter except for the snow drifting over a dog curled in a hollow with his tail protecting his nose. Not even penguins and seals could survive out on the ice in winter. This dog was one of the two huge French-Canadian Shambouls, so powerful that I had driven the two, with only one other dog in the team, for several weeks the previous summer.

More than one week after his departure, Toby returned to the base camp thinner and wiser, in good health and spirits. How far away he had run we had no way of knowing.

Had he known all the time which way the base lay, so that he could have chosen to return at any time?

33

RACHEL CARSON AND THE MODERN ENVIRONMENTAL MOVEMENT

AN UNSCRUPULOUS, conscienceless woman who wrote a false and sensational book solely to make money from gullible readers. This was the characterization of biologist Rachel Carson presented by a speaker, who was later to become a Cabinet member in a federal administration, during a public meeting in 1963 devoted solely to denouncing the book *Silent Spring*.

The storm that raged over this beautifully written popularization was not a scientific controversy, but one of public policy over indiscriminate use of biocides. Probably the most criticized part of the book was her warning against the (now thoroughly proven) general hazard of environmental carcinogens, so that her early death from cancer was both tragic and ironic. The short-term damage to the author's reputation which the controversy caused in many quarters in the Sixties has been more than compensated since her death as the full meaning of her work has sunk into public consciousness, and the weight of personal sacrifice she suffered by "committing the truth" is coming to be widely appreciated.

Other shy, retiring thinkers have also played leading roles in changing the world. Charles Darwin's *Origin of Species* and Karl Marx's *Das Kapital* are recognized as the two most fateful books, for better or worse, of the nineteenth century. Like Darwin, Miss Carson hated controversy. The next-to-last and most influential of her five books first convinced the thinking public that Nature is a seamless web of interrelationships and that Man is part of and dependent upon the ecosystems of life. The television documentary "debate" presented by Eric Sevareid focused on the pesticide issue, and had much impact in making her views respectable for the public. But this was merely one of three levels covered in *Silent Spring*. The second was the issue of environmental pollution in general, which was beginning to come to the fore during that decade. Third, and most important, was the first successful introduction into public thought of ecosystem ideas, an integrated picture of the Earth as a whole which was buttressed by seeing the planet from Space through the Apollo flights.

Books are undeniably highly influential for molding belief and behavior. In our century, *Mein Kampf* was an important book, but negatively so. *Silent Spring* changed the mind-set of society in a vital and positive way. It should prove to be one of the most influential of recent books if its message continues to be heeded. If not, Heaven help us!

When Carson's book appeared in 1962, people were increasingly concerned about pollution of air, water, and land by industry, agriculture and transportation, and about "inner-space pollution" from burgeoning populations and urban metastasis. But these worries, justified as far as they went, were not seen in the proper conceptual context. Thus they were shallowed by having little philosophical underpinning. Carson showed humanity as a whole what ecological scientists had long known—where we stand in the big picture, the planetary ecosystem wherein the natural scheme of things is the basic underlying reality.

Among my most cherished possessions is a January 21, 1963, letter from Rachel Carson. A public-relations office of one man and eight secretaries, with a high-sounding name, was flooding the country with leaflets attacking *Silent Spring*. From the standpoint of a professional ecologist, I wrote this front group my analysis of its materials, and sent a copy of my letter to Carson. Her reply follows.

I was of course delighted with every word in your

letter to the [Bleep—Bleep]. I have been aware for several weeks that this material was going out on various mailing lists and it now seems clear that it is going to the universities as well. I sincerely appreciate your fine defense of my position and your very able pointing out of the weaknesses in the stand taken by this industry-sponsored organization.

Considerably later, at the instigation of the Save The Dunes Council, I tried to interest her in writing a book on the effort to set up an Indiana Dunes National Lakeshore, offering her my collection of documents, correspondence, reprints, and clippings on this conservation cliffhanger. Miss Carson explained that she whole-heartedly supported the Council, but that publishing commitments for the future would not leave time for the work. We were not aware that she was then in a bout with cancer; this became generally known only after her death. My papers on the Lakeshore effort, which started in 1952 again after lying dormant since 1917, are now in the Calumet Regional Archives of Indiana University Northwest.

Tides of environmental action have flowed and ebbed, but there have been only two tsunamis. The first of these tidal waves was inaugurated chiefly by Theodore Roosevelt and his (mostly hunter) friends in the first decade of this century. By the Forties, the environmental issue had largely faded out of public consciousness, except for the interest in soil conservation stemming from the Dust Bowl during the great depression. General environmentalism was kept smoldering during the Forties and Fifties by an "underground" of writer-ecologists. Fairfield Osborn and William Vogt wrote important books. Professors Aldo Leopold and Paul Sears were mainly research ecologists; both served as presidents of the professional group Ecological Society of America. Professors and other teachers recognized that the chief responsibility of education is to enable educated citizens to transcend the hogwash.

The second major wave of environmental concern began

with Rachel Carson's 1962 book and came to fruition in the Seventies. It is now necessary to defend the gains made then, and not allow the Eighties to be remembered as the decade of the Great Terrain Robbery.

Carson loved the sea and its life; she wrote about them in three enduring books that were typical of her in being non-controversial. Three appropriate physical memorials to her are strips of shoreline preserved in natural condition. One is preserved as the Rachel Carson National Wildlife Refuge near Kennebunkport, Maine, and another section of Maine coast is held by The Nature Conservancy in her memory. Funds are being raised by Duke University to buy a coastal area near Beaufort NC where she worked in the summer of 1949. More meaningful even, than such Nature Preserves honoring her, is that Carson's principles be disseminated, and applied in action.

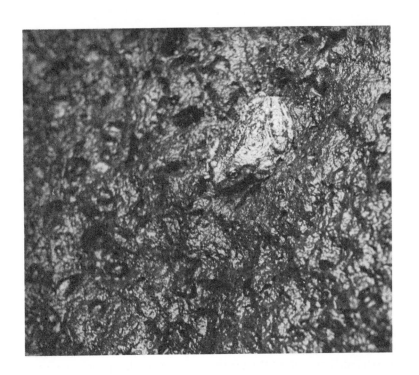

34

PROTECTIVE COLORATION IN
DESERT LIFE

THAT tropical birds are flamboyantly colored is common knowledge. Many frogs in the Tropical Moist Forest are equally so. In Costa Rica, we found such frogs quiescent and absurdly easy to photograph. Two species, an inch to an inch and a half long, allow themselves to be picked up. Not with my bare hands, though, for the scarlet and black species and the green and black one are poison-arrow frogs, their skin toxins used by primitive Indians. To any predator not color-blind, their brilliant coloration calls attention to their presence, but no animal bites into either of these species a second time. They represent color and pattern devoted to a warning function.

At La Selva in the Atlantic coastal wet forest, a botanist friend went out with a flashlight to spot bizarre tropical insects on the dense wall of foliage bordering the clearing around our cottage laboratory. Instead of insects, he at once brought back a hand-size frog he had picked off a large leaf, its pattern conspicuous with piebald yellow and black. It proved, despite the casual capture, to be a species new to science!

In contrast to much brightly colored life in the tropics, desert animals, like desert landscape, tend to be dun and dull. They represent the concealing, not the revealing, type of coloration.

Looking for unusual lichens, mosses or ferns in a desert wilderness of black lava, I lowered myself into a deep, dim fissure. Only a close examination of its vertical wall revealed a frog, considerably larger than our tree frogs but with expanded, clinging toes. With darkly variegated color pattern, it perfectly matched the appearance of the lava rock where it remained persistently immobile. This frog's "faith" was in its invisibility granted by its evolution in that special habitat, not in poison glands in its skin.

During five years of frequent field trips to this Grants, N.M., lava terrain, only two of these lava-mimics were seen. It seems quite possible that this frog is still undescribed, but, rare as it seems to be, I collected none, preferring not to contribute to an extinction by contributing to science at that frog's expense.

In the hotter, dryer climate of southeastern New Mexico lies the long black band of the Carrizozo Lava Bed. Not too surprisingly, the species of mouse which successfully occupies this habitat is black like its background. Predators have insured the supremacy of the black population over lighter competitors. Nearby is an extensive barren region of exposed red sandstone, which supports mice with rufous pelage. A better-known area near the other two is White Sands National Monument; its sand is pulverized white gypsum instead of silica. The mice there are white. This tripartite contrast furnishes classical evidence for the theory of protective resemblance. Theodore Roosevelt, from his vast field experience throughout the world, wrote a 126-page monograph on the subject, published by the American Museum of Natural History. Zealous claims by artist Abbott Thayer emphasizing the concealment function of color had precipitated a controversy which this work by TR helped to settle. He recognized both concealing and revealing coloration as valid, and distinguished clearly between them.

About the time when zoologist William Koster and I trapped for white mice at White Sands, there was a new flurry about protective coloration. Some laboratory-bound theorists claimed that it was a pigment of the imagination. A few years later, a splendid big book by a British zoologist named Cott thoroughly confirmed its reality. Cott's treatment was more technical and up to date than the perceptive explanations and observations of Roosevelt and other experienced field men. It put a definite end to the simple protective coloration controversies. The marvels of its perfection are still with us.

Green plants, whose business requires exposure to light, would not be expected to illustrate protective resemblance. But among the low-growing "belly plants" of southern California deserts is a small species of *Gilia* which does so. The narrow, thread-like leaves are too inconspicuous to show against the desert floor; however, it is the flowers that are really remarkable. When open, they are white and an inch in diameter. If open during daytime, they would merely attract grazing animals, for their pollinating insects fly at night. In daylight, the flower is twisted spirally into a slender bud-like structure that matches the color of the gray sandy substrate where the plant grows. How can white petals seem to be a dull gray during daylight hours? Only on one edge of only the underside of each petal is there a one-eighth-inch border of the dark tone. When light has stimulated the petals to twist together and close the flower, only that narrow crescent on what has become the *outside* edge of each petal is exposed, so that no white is seen. At twilight the tightly twisted, inconspicuous "bud" rapidly unfurls. The desert floor suddenly explodes with the white blossoms that attract night-flying pollinators.

The most specialized case of resemblance in animals that I have documented photographically is that of a rare horned lizard living only among rounded light-gray pebbles of the dry desert washes. Koster and I were delighted to encounter this small "horned toad" in southern New Mexico. Had it not been moving, we would never have detected it.

The lizard is exactly the same color and tone on its upper surface as the pebbles. It does not conform to the well-known principle of counter-shading by being lighter underneath. Instead, its pattern blends into the stark pattern of contrasting brightness and shade among the small pebbles. On each side of its body is a black, sharply delimited patch that simulated the dark shadow on the unlighted side and bottom of a pebble of the uniform size found in the habitat. As long as the little fellow remains motionless, it is practically impossible to spot him in the first place. In fact, I had set up my tripod and camera within a couple of feet of the trusting reptile and taken one picture. When I looked away momentarily, neither of us having moved otherwise, I could not see him again until I looked through the view-finder to spot where he was sitting, still in the center of the frame.

Despite the background being a highly special one, there is at least this one creature adapted to blend into it. It is tempting to expand the dictum "Nature abhors a vacuum" by adding, "and to fill it uses just about every trick imaginable."

Dr. Edmund C. Jaeger of Riverside College was unsurpassed in his knowledge of the southern California deserts.

The match in coloring between the plumage of a Poor-will cramped into a small rock-cavity and the rock's color was not so perfect but that Jaeger made a discovery far more exciting than protective resemblance. It was winter, and the bird was torpid, with a much-lowered body temperature—the first known case of hibernation in birds. His find illustrates the First Law of Serendipity, which holds that to discover anything you must first be looking for something.

35

THE FIRST ASCENT OF MOUNT CITADEL

ALTHOUGH this planet offers more stupendous mountain vistas, there is one view which to me is surpassingly beautiful—the intimate mountain and lake scene at Saint Mary's Lake on the east side of our Glacier National Park, Montana. At the southeast foot of bright and stately Going-to-the-Sun Mountain, the visitor may pull into a large paved area along the shore. Across the lake from there, rising abruptly from waters colored green by "glacial flour," rose-tinted peaks march in close order drill toward the continental divide on the western skyline. It is a rare day when their cliffs are not salted with a sprinkling of white mountain goats.

I regard as one of the highest rewards of an outdoor life the privilege of working as a park service ranger-naturalist upon and beside this inspiring lake in the summer of 1939. My headquarters was at delightful Going-to-the-Sun Chalet, of which nothing remains today except that parking lot on the site where the Swiss-style Chalet then stood.

Indians knew Saint Mary's as "Old Woman Lake," because of nearly constant westerlies sweeping down the lake from the continent's crest-line, whipping up waves whose foaming white tops were reminiscent of white hair. The centerpiece of the inimitable scene is precipitous Mount Citadel or Dusty Star rising just to the south of Saint Mary's inlet. It is a peak of distinctive double form and near-perfect symmetry. During the infrequent calm moods of the lake waters, its sharply etched reflection completes an unforgettable picture.

Mount Citadel had never been climbed! This was the

challenging news brought by ranger-naturalist Jim Dyson. That geologist and mountaineer had searched the records thoroughly, and was certain that if we made the climb we would find no cairn left by previous climbers. Jim proposed that three of us with mountaineering experience should try the peak soon. The third man would be Roland Everson, who manned the information desk at the Chalet lobby. It would be a one-day climb, but an extremely long day from the Chalet base. I suspected that before it was over the perpetual grin might temporarily come off the face of cheerful Jim Dyson.

After leaving the Chalet hours before first light, we rapidly covered the trail along the north lakeshore. Those two tall, long-legged fellows were somewhat stronger hikers than I, but I had to keep up throughout this venture. At length we struck off through the trackless conifer forest toward the base of Citadel. The approach constantly steepened, and when full daylight arrived we were still climbing "hand over hand," clutching the crowded trunks of spruces to pull ourselves from tree to tree up a punishing slope. On an earlier day, we had scouted that slope from a distance through binoculars; the densely packed forest when seen reduced by distance gave us the impression of a solid growth of erect mosses on a steep-sided boulder.

This mountain has the form of an overstuffed chair with a relatively low back curving down on the east and west sides to high arms facing the head of the lake. A colossal glacial cirque, nearly empty of ice now in July, is encircled on three sides by the chair's back and arms, suggesting the gently sloping seat of the rocky armchair. After an exhausting period of the unorthodox climbing technique, we came up to the thin woods and easier going of the chair's seat, opening toward the lake's head. As we headed southeast to push diagonally up the talus slope of the east arm, it became more open and rocky as it steepened. Dark brown argyllite rocks predominated.

179

Across the valley to our north loomed colorful Going-to-the-Sun, flaunting its red and green argyllite, consolidated from ocean-deposited clays. Higher up the peak, massive limestone cliffs are shot through with broad bands of once-molten intrusives, the original heat of which metamorphosed the sedimentary limestone to a pair of conspicuous bands of marble, one below and one above the intrusive dike. With but a modicum of geological background, he who runs may read the history of drastic changes reflected now in sharply contrasting coloring. On earlier trips up the Sun trail from the Chalet, I had photographed the large-scale folding of the rock strata that occurred when the mountain-building block was shoved over the top of the crust on the east side of the fault line. This great overthrust fault which reared the front range of the Rockies generated the pressure that crumpled the strata, at one point that I photographed, so that they appeared S-shaped in section.

From our angle of view from Citadel, Sun Peak did not show the familiar snow and rock pattern just below its summit that one sees clearly while driving toward the peak from some distance southeast of it. This is readily recognizable as a snowy white head of an Indian wearing a feathered war bonnet; it can be seen when one is still many miles away from the mountain.

On striking the ascending ridge-top of the east arm of Citadel, we followed up its spine as it headed first southward and then curved around to our right toward the conical low summit on the "back" of the armchair. Looking down into the deep, wide valley between us and the mountain farther east, a valley which hikers rarely penetrated, we saw far away a large herd of elk. These were the first wild elk I had seen, and remain the only ones I have seen in any national park except Yellowstone and the Tetons. Unlike the Jackson Hole herd, the Glacier elk were reputed to be extremely wary and generally successful in keeping out of man's sight. Those we saw were probably unaware of the three moving projections against their distant skyline.

Keeping always to the high line of the ridge as we ascended, we finally were close enough to the summit to look for a possible cairn. This was a case of looking hard for something which we did not want to find, for it would have shown that we were not the first climbers atop Citadel Mountain. At the summit we found no evidence whatsoever of a cairn or any disturbance by humans. Apparently the resentful mountains did not want man there, in one of their few remaining untrod sanctuaries, for we found it very difficult to keep our footing against the cold force of a vengeful gale. Between bouts of shivering and arm-swinging, we wrote out the date, time, and our names, and placed the record of this first ascent in a watertight container. We built a sturdy and conspicuous rock-cairn over it on the 9,024-foot high point of Mount Citadel.

Dyson had planned and led the climb. It had not been a technical one, and we had not needed to rope ourselves together, but this day was a test of endurance. At last, during the return trek when I had to stretch to the utmost to keep up with the other two on the trail in darkness, Jim's usual bubbling buoyancy had deserted him. Arriving back at the Chalet at 10:30, we could look back on more than a grueling, exhausting day of constant action. We had seen the magnificent skyline of the eastern Rockies as no white man, and probably no human being, had ever seen it before.

Some years after, I found a new book entitled "Ice" which was written by James Dyson, head of the geology department at Lafayette College. Still later, we met quite by accident in the corridor of Dr. John Marr's Alpine Research Station of the University of Colorado. Though neither of us had been expected, Marr invited us to join that day's excursion to the high tundra on the ridge behind the station. This proved by far the roughest ride either of us had known in any vehicle. In a highly specialized and powerful truck with high, boulder-clearing axles, we were carried on a long, direct course straight up the rough mountainside for miles.

Thus I got to spend a second day with Jim Dyson on a mountain. We tramped through the extensive tundra community from which we could see Boulder far away. The researchers explained their experiments on the ground there, in this typical tundra of our northern Rockies, remote from tourists, where the ecologists were utilizing its research possibilities to the full. However, most impressive to me was the conspicuous system of bare "stone stripes," a rare sight better exemplified here than anywhere I had seen in Arctic Canada. Each stripe in the series was a low ridge of boulders lacking plant cover. Stone stripes represent a numerous and extremely varied class of phenomena caused by frost action and common in arctic and alpine terrain.

Of the national parks in the conterminous United States, the two in which I have been employed best illustrate glaciation. Glacier National Park has some small living glaciers, but is remarkable for its varied evidences of past glaciation, whereas Mount Rainier has our greatest system of living glaciers outside of Alaska.

My friend Jim Dyson is gone now, and I am probably the only person who regards Mount Citadel as a memorial to him and his way of life in science and exploration in the beauty spots of Nature nearer home. Mount Citadel is not Mount Everest or Kanchenjunga, but we three were happy to make the first ascent of that lovely and familiar peak which climaxes a lake-mountain scene beloved of thousands.

36

THE TOP OF THE MORNING

BECAUSE the boys of the Civilian Conservation Corps (CCC) had worked hard all summer improving forest trails and building rustic footbridges at Mount Rainier National Park, they deserved some sort of bonus. The park superintendent offered them a free climactic adventure before they returned, hardened physically and mellowed spiritually, to their homes in the Lower East Side of New York. Those who wished could tackle the summit climb in the care of a few rangers and ranger-naturalists and led by now-famed Rainier ranger Bill Butler. I was one of those assigned to this ascent of September 1-2, 1933.

Our party left Paradise Ranger Station in early afternoon, and a leisurely climb up the lower snow slope brought us at 6:30 to the two stone huts constituting Camp Muir. At this site in 1888, John Muir's party of nine had huddled over-night behind rocks, sleepless in wind too strong to permit fires. James Longmire had packed them in by way of Soda Springs (Longmire WA) to Cloud Camp (Paradise Valley) where the horses were left. This became the third successful climb to Rainier's summit, and it was guided by the same Van Trump who, with the governor's son Hazard Stevens, had in 1872 made the first one. The noted geologist Ingraham was along with Muir, also photographer Arthur C. Warner who was the first person to take a camera to the summit. He made negatives on sheet film rather than glass, the first ever used in the Pacific Northwest.

Weather prospects for the next day looked favorable, and at 8:30 we turned in. Each bed, exactly four feet wide, was occupied by two men. A safe climbing schedule allowed only two hours of rest here; I and most others slept only forty-five minutes. Camp Muir is at the 10,000 foot level, perched on the cleaver between the Nisqually and Cowlitz Glaciers on the southeast flank of the old volcano. On the Gibraltar Rock trail which we were to follow (but which is today impassable because the narrow ledge has fallen away), pebbles would begin to hurtle bullet-like from the precipice above as soon as the morning sun struck the frozen cliff-face. Before that hap-pened, we had to traverse the ledge on our *return* from the summit. This necessitated a night climb going up the moun-tain.

The narrow Cowlitz Cleaver was bare of snow, and sloped steeply upward like the crest-line of a dinosaur's back. We headed up it from Camp Muir by the bright light of a perfectly full moon. Our caulked boots struck profuse sparks from the dark volcanic rock; with the climbers well ahead hardly visible against the dark shadows, the effect was that of a flight of fireflies strung out in long formation up the steep mountainside. Below us stretched a vast fairyland under the moon. The lights of Paradise gleamed far beneath us at the edge of a billowy ocean of white clouds that filled the world to its own far horizon to the south and west. The cloud mass reached up to the 5,500-foot level when we left Muir, slowly settling lower as the night progressed. The minor mountain range closest to the south, the Tatoosh, thrust many peaks above the brilliant white-caps of the cloud sea like a string of black, disconnected islands. Farther peaks and ranges were larger islands and archipelagos as far as the eye could reach. At first the night was calm and chilly, but soon we had to adjust our parka hoods against a stiff breeze.

By 2:40 AM we had attained Camp Misery, where we snacked on chocolate and raisins, lying flat against the rock ridge for protection from the blast of wind-driven pumice sand. The CCC fellows had no crampons; the others put theirs on for the ice was ahead. The party was roped together in three lines. Soon we started the hands-knees crawl and belly-creep along the face of Gibraltar's notorious precipice on a rising ledge only eighteen inches wide, overhanging and overhung by tremendous cliffs. Then along the angled base of the Rock's upper end to "The Chutes." One Triple-C boy had come down with mountain sickness, so that we made frequent pauses on the Chutes on his account. Several times he decided to quit at the next possible stopping point, but he never did. Others of his mates and one Park Service man dropped out at Camp Comfort above Gibraltar to await the party on its return trip.

The Chutes furnished safe going, for the ice was deeply and thoroughly honeycombed, leaving great pinnacles that were difficult to traverse but would have stopped any man who lost his footing from sliding down the mountainside. Night still prevailed as we threaded our way through the waist-high ice-pinnacles, but soon the East became streaked. Before and long after the sun became visible at 5:30, the sky was glorious with red and gold throughout. The then symmetric cone of Mount Saint Helens shone rose-pink to the south. A sunrise of such wide scope was unprecedented in the experience of any of us there. As it faded, we were making the long, steep pull to the summit on slopes where climbers foolish enough to sit down have shot to their deaths below. This part of the climb was a smooth one except for three bad crevasses which the roped groups crossed on dangerously thin snow-bridges.

The sick chap got sicker and sicker. Three other CCC boys quit before crossing the highest and worst crevasse, and an NPS man guided them back to Camp Comfort. Seven of the dozen boys who had started, plus Butler, Buckmaster and I, reached the rim of the summit crater at 7:10 AM. After signing the Mountaineers Club record at Register Rock, we unroped, and those who wished could walk around independently on the reasonably safe dome of snow around the shallow crater. Eating our sandwiches on the literal run to save precious time, three of us pantingly reached the top-most point of the highest volcano in the contiguous United States. The clear view in all directions from the summit was not really "out of this world." It *was* this world! And we had fully earned the right to see it.

Two ropes, five men each; this time I was first in our line. Butler's line crept down the steep side of the summit dome first. We all got to Camp Comfort with no more serious event than the loss of an alpenstock by one of Bill's charges. It sped down the dome to the edge of a crevasse where it stuck in the snow. The line of men cautiously swung around so the one at the lower end could be held leaning over the crevasse while he retrieved it.

Having left the crater rim at 8:20 AM, we reached Comfort at 9:35 and picked up into our roped lines all the rest except the sick man left at Misery lower down. We ate a snack at Comfort, then followed on our bellies the downward pitch along Gibraltar's terrifying ledge, watching for rockslides and listening for pebble-bullets from above. A few small slides occurred, but not near enough to cause concern. The Gibraltar ledge on the old standard route above Paradise Valley gave the strongest flavor of hazard-spice to the ascent;

its loss to weathering and gravity has made the average modern climb of Rainier much less thrilling.

Descending the steep rocky pitch of Cowlitz Cleaver, I was bothered by a stiffness and soreness in my left hip, and even more by the nails sticking up into my feet from the Company boots. At about 1:00 PM at Camp Muir, we enjoyed soup, the first hot food or drink since we had left Muir on the upward trek. Two of us rode the wind and ice axes down the mountainside as far as it remained steep enough.

A few weeks later, I was helping to load Byrd's flagship at Boston Navy Yard, for a near two-year antarctic expedition before going back to Rainier for the summer of 1935.

37

TIME AND THE MOUNTAIN

A SENSE of time is feared and rejected by some, but others cherish it as adding a revealing dimension to observations and thought. Four decades is a brief moment in the history of a mountain like Rainier, but it is long enough to see striking changes in the plant cover, and even in landforms related to glacial ice and running water.

We eagerly returned to the old park for the summer of 1974; in fact, I retired at sixty-seven in order to spend this fourth summer there while still able to climb to Camp Muir within 4,400 feet of the summit, and we did this. My hobby that summer was to rephotograph the sites of as many as possible of my hundreds of landscape pictures taken forty-one years before. This was to demonstrate change over time, or, as sometimes proved just as interesting, absence of change. The element of the landscape that interested me most was the vegetation. Vegetation (true fir forest, alpine tundra, etc.) is the display that the plant life of an area makes collectively. This display is not determined by the species flora as a whole, but by the dominant or controlling species. In a forest, of course, these are the largest and most abundant trees. Ecologists are most interested in vegetation, whereas taxonomists (systematists) are most concerned with the entire list of plants present, and especially intrigued by the rare species, but not by the way the community and ecosystem are organized and function.

Relocating the sites proved much easier than expected, and the photography was accomplished in nine weeks. Once we had hiked to the general vicinity, I would hold up a 5″ ×

7 " print of the original picture, and, by triangulating prominent features in the background or on the skyline, I would move in the direction that brought the real scene in conformity with the old photo, and take a new picture there. In some cases, because of changes in stream courses and flood plain structure, or glacial ice which had dumped morainal rock-piles, the place I had stood years before no longer existed.

Rainier's glaciers have been receding through excess of melting over accumulation ever since white men first saw them at close range. My friend Len Longmire was the first to detect the recession. Continued glacial recession had brought about obvious changes since my 1933 pictures. A photo-pair taken up the Nisqually Glacier from the summit of Eagle Peak shows the further retreat of that glacier's snout position, and lowering of its general surface.

I recalled that many early Saturdays and Sundays had found me at this glacier's rock-strewn terminus, explaining glacial action to those who hiked up the trail from the highway bridge. By now, however, much of the former flood plain has been washed out and the trail with it. No trail is now maintained because the snout is so much farther up the mountain that few would hike to it.

The next day, I beat my way up through the tangled alders, jumping from great raw boulder to boulder, to the position the snout had occupied in 1933. From there no snout was to be seen, for it had retreated upstream around a bend in the hill on the west side of the valley. All the valley within sight had been liberated from the ice which had filled it above the point where I stood. Recalling the high, lost ice cliff that I had known so well, I realized that a glacier shares with an old tree the power to catch and encapsulate time. The earliest time found in a tree is in the pith and innermost heartwood. In a glacier, the snows of the more remote yesteryears became the ice farthest down the valley, at the terminus. The snout fills the valley from wall to wall with ice that looks as black and shiny and moist as a dog's nose.

As long as that oldest ice remains unmelted, all the years when the snows collected higher up are preserved. The years and the memories of their events slowly run together, flow gradually downslope, where they eventually melt away and dissipate seaward. The damp, cold glacier-snout exposes the earliest years that the existing glacier contains, but as soon as the ice thaws the memories are released, becoming warm and surrounded only by the transparent body of a spectral glacier. Through this I could see upgrade into the bedrock valley beyond. Perhaps this is where all our old campfires went when they died.

For pioneer Len Longmire, this ghost glacier extended much farther down the valley than it does for me, but it reaches farther down for me than for younger visitors to this valley. Once I wondered whether a close inspection of the phantom ice would reveal a rakish foot, shod in the leather ranger-boot of a bygone day, projecting from the imaginary ice-front. If I were to step through that time warp and walk up the valley beyond it, would I again be the same person as when I was living through it all? Of course I shall have changed considerably from infancy through senility in the real world, but which part of that changing continuum represents the real me? Does anyone expect to find Heaven occupied, like many Florida towns, largely by senior citizens?

With a good series of old photos of timberline tree forms in our backpacks, my wife and I climbed Burroughs Mountain where they had been taken in 1941. We found all of the same trees within a few hundred yards of the trail, and took new pictures which demonstrate that all survived. But there has been remarkably little of either growth of new wood or decline through dying back of branchlets. The later photos are almost interchangable with the earlier ones for a given tree, family group, or prostrate mat.

Burroughs Mountain is one of the larger exposed roots of the battered stump that is Mount Rainier, or what is left of the original Mount Rainier. It lies on the northeast or Sunrise side of the volcano, between the Emmons and Winthrop Glaciers. Originally its name was John Burroughs Mountain. That literary-naturalist never glimpsed Rainier, for it was hidden by a cloud-shroud while he was in Seattle enroute to and from Alaska in 1899. No one knows why, how, or by whom the mountain was named for him. I suspect that his friend Muir had something to do with it. Far vaster scenic features were named for both of them to commemorate their visit to Alaska with Harriman—the Muir Glacier and adjacent Burroughs Glacier at Glacier Bay National Park in a sense parallel Camp Muir and Burroughs Mountain on the slopes of Rainier.

Our fellow camper that '74 summer, nephew Frank Levering, had been brought up on his parents' orchard in Virginia's Blue Ridge. Although he had climbed Long's Peak in the Rockies, he was not comfortable with a mountain of Rainier's grandeur. Because of the snow-enhanced beauty remaining from the highly excessive snowfall of the previous winter, Frank and I wanted to see the Queen in her longest, whitest gown and to watch the changing patterns of shadow and color throughout many day and night hours. The ideal place for this is the fire lookout tower atop Gobblers Knob; it allows an unobstructed view from high up and only eight miles horizontal measure from Rainier's summit. The tower is no longer used for reporting forest fires, but on summer week-ends a ranger is stationed there to explain to climbers how it can be done where needed.

With a key and permission from headquarters, we hiked up past the lovely shimmering jewel called Lake George and through fir forest and exfoliated old snow to the knob's peak. The diverging glacial tentacles of The Mountain separated the upreaching, converging fingers formed by forested ridges. Seen thus at close hand with perfect lighting, Rainier was a colossal diamond in an emerald setting.

The cabin capping the tower is a square box of ample size, with glass windows on the four sides. In order to be uniquely focused on the awesome view to the east, we lifted and secured the large dark shutter from the glass wall on that side only. The effect was startling, for the glass walls of the three sides still darkened by their closed shutters were splendid mirrors.

As we disposed of our evening meal and spread our sleeping bags on the floor, the real Mount Rainier to the east and its snowy support system surrounded us on all sides with its repetitive mural. We were, through the remaining daylight and the half-darkness of night, dwarfed and overpowered within our isolated glass box by the immaculate peak in its unprecedented majesty. It was not at all the potential for an eruption that got to us—it was the presence itself. Nature's silent, eloquent representative evoked not a commonplace sense of humility, but a deep-seated and little understood slow fear such as neither of us had known before.

38

THE RECORD TREES OF THE MIDWEST

COULD it be possible that the flood plain forests which occupied the southern Wabash valley into the 1880s were as impressive as the tropical rain forests of Central America?

The equality of these two forests was clearly documented by an early Smithsonian biologist, by extensive measurements and photographs. The evidence came down to me through a "mental food-chain" of four steps from the "producer," Robert Ridgway.

Ridgway was an old-style, self-made naturalist whose youth was spent in Mount Carmel, Illinois, a river town. He also lived in Wheatland, Indiana. As a young man he accompanied the famed Hayden Expedition, one of the scientifically important Army excursions through the old West. He did much biological collecting in Central America also, and in 1899 was recruited with thirty top-flight professionals to serve as ornithologist on the celebrated Harriman Alaska Expedition (Chapter 18 herein).

The Charles C. Deam Wilderness, established in southern Indiana in 1982, is named in memory of the great Hoosier botanist and conservationist. Deam and Ridgway were close friends. In 1919, Ridgway sent to Deam for safekeeping a set of remarkable photographs and factual legends made during his thorough study of Wabash flood plain trees about 1885, in Indiana and Illinois.

Soon before Deam's death at eighty-seven, Deam turned the material over to a friend who taught forestry courses. Very few of the pictures had been published in Ridgway's seven papers on this tree work in National Museum Reports and technical journals. I was working on a five-year project on Wabash-Tippecanoe forests, and borrowed the set from Deam's friend, publishing three of the photos in Ecological Monographs, April 1951 issue. Another is presented in the chapter-head illustration above; the man at the left is Robert Ridgway, probably before he became a department head at the U. S. National Museum.

I relocated the point from which Ridgway had photographed from a bluff the flood plain forest near the mouth of the White River. The unbroken line of tree-tops on the Indiana side which his photo shows has given way to a ragged line with numerous openings. Ridgway had described the scene as ". . . a compact level sea of green, apparently almost endless, . . . the general level broken by occasional giant trees." The latter were mainly cypresses and tulip trees.

By triangulation of standing trees and taping of fallen ones, Ridgway determined the average tree-top level as 130 feet. The "by no means infrequent monarchs attained more than 180 feet," and the sycamores and tulip trees approached 200 feet closely. In one picture of a cluster of four tulip trees near Vincennes in 1888, the trunks ranged from five to seven feet in diameter. "The following year I revisited the locality and all these trees had been cut." One photograph shows a man standing with his hand on a pin oak. From the probable height of the man, I scaled off a distance of seventy-eight feet of trunk from the ground upward to the first branch, practically without trunk taper. The greatest diameter he measured for a tulip tree was eleven feet, but the cut surface of a stump measured twelve feet in diameter. The average of twenty-five standing tulip trees he taped was 6.2 feet.

A Shumard's red oak he photographed below the mouth of the White River was six feet in diameter at twelve feet up, and the base itself was twelve feet across. He noted that within a hundred yards of this oak were two black walnut trees, each six feet in diameter above the butt swell. (In 1976 a black walnut tree near Pioneer in Ohio sold for $30,000.)

All the Ridgway trees thus far were on the high bottom or second terrace of the Wabash. On first bottoms, and especially in swamps, the bald cypress would be considered giants today but were passed over as too small in the lumbering.

Ridgway described Little Cypress Swamp across the river from Mount Carmel as comprising twenty thousand acres. He commented that the finer trees had been rafted away for shingles, and that the remnant was undoubtedly a poor sample from which to judge the character of the original forest stand. "Certain it is that several stumps, where cut off at the beginning of the cylindrical section, measured nine and ten feet across. . . . Some of those felled far exceeded in dimensions any now standing."

The picture of one living cypress which he labelled "*Average* size mature *Taxodium*" shows a man beside the trunk, enabling me to scale its diameter above the butt swell as seven feet. Only one of the many cypresses I have taped in Indiana had as large a size. His "average" specimen was the mean of mature trees left after the ones big enough to be "worth cutting" had already been removed.

I have no doubt that Ridgway was justified in comparing this midwestern timber with the tropical rain forest, which I also have studied in Costa Rica. His photographs of huge tulip trees, oaks, sycamores, and ash trees tell a story of potential hardwood tree sizes for us moderns who consider a tree of three feet in diameter as very large indeed.

39

WITNESS FOR THE DEFENSE

WHETHER Miss Beall of Mount Carmel, Illinois, had ever heard of former townsman Robert Ridgway and his early work on the antique forests along the Wabash River nearby I do not know. But she did know that the virgin forest she owned eight miles south of town was far too important as a historical and scientific rarity to ever allow cutting.

Keeping this remarkable stand of trees inviolate had been a long-standing tradition in the Beall family. The last of her line, Miss Beall (pronounced "Bell") remained unmarried, and preserving the 279-acre woods along the lower reach of Sugar Creek where it joins the Wabash became the major devotion of her long life.

Hearing rumors of an outstanding forest near Keensburg village, I searched it out in the spring of 1961, accompanied by plant ecologist Elroy Rice of Oklahoma. We recognized at once the "Ridgway caliber" of Beall Woods. Soon I returned to carry out a detailed sampling study; my analysis was published in the Indiana Academy of Science Proceedings for 1962. Since Illinois was then one of only eight states having a nature preservation law, I believed there was a chance to preserve this stand, the very last example of the extraordinary flood plain forests which had been described by Ridgway while they were still extant.

As part of settling the Beall estate after Miss Beall's death, the forest was put up for tax sale. Neither the Illinois Department of Natural Resources nor the state's chapter of The Nature Conservancy were able to move quickly enough to save it. The property was bought for a song by an elderly man who expressed his determination to cut off the timber. When the state approached with an offer to pay him the appraised value of $200,000. in order to set up a state nature preserve, he declined to sell it for any figure.

A condemnation case was heard at the courthouse in Mount Carmel on February 15, 1965. Preservationist George Collins came from California in order to testify on the principle of preserving outdoor museum-pieces of a value far surpassing the current commercial one. Professor Charles Olmsted of the University of Chicago botany department came with Mr. Jeffrey Short, a Chicago industrialist who was making a serious hobby of studying trees throughout the world. My wife and I found this experience in which Nature herself was on trial to be a most interesting one. I was on the witness stand, in defense of the last Ridgway-type forest, for eighty minutes, since I was more familiar with the woods than anyone else. The state's attorney, Mr. Crain, skillfully questioned me so as to bring out the crucial points. This is part of the court record:

Q. Tell the Court what you did in your study upon the premises of Beall Woods.
A. I measured all trees in the . . . plots that were four inches in diameter and larger, both in the bottomland and upland portions. I treated them as two distinct forest types.
Q. Will you tell the Court the difference . . .?
A. Due to the difference in drainage conditions, the bottomland forest, which is quite comparable to that which Ridgway described while he lived here in Mt. Carmel, has distinct species composition. It contains huge Shumard red oaks, elms, sycamores and sweet gums. The number and size of the sweet gums are almost unbelievable. In the upland, though, only a few feet higher, you find an oak-hickory-maple type. The upland stand contains thirty tree species, and by coincidence the low-ground stand also has thirty species, the

dominant ones sweet gums, wetland oaks, and elm. Are you ready for me to show this?

Q. Yes.

Forest Stands	Square Inches Basal Area	Number of Stems per Acre
Beall Woods IL		
Bottomland	199	114.5
Upland	152	115
Allee Memorial Forest IN	145	107
Hoot Woods IN	136	73
Donaldson's Woods, (Spring Mill St. Pk., IN)	125	123

A. (Showing placard to Court) This is a comparison of the best virgin stands in Indiana with both the upland and bottomland of the Beall Woods stands. The first column of figures shows the basal area per average acre of all tree species combined, and the other is the number of trees, or total density of all species combined, on the average acre. Now here is Donaldson's Woods in southern Indiana, considered our most impressive stand of virgin timber in Indiana, with a basal area of 125 square feet per acre. One can picture what the figure means if you think of a stand of timber cut down at the 4.5-foot level, cutting every tree at least four inches in diameter, and then measure the area of the flat tops of the stumps. This gives an excellent idea of the quality of the stand. At Beall, the upland gives a higher basal area than any of the other upland woods, but the Beall bottomland at 199 sq. ft. is just phenomenal. I know of no other stand in the eastern U.S. that approaches this. Now density has to be interpreted in the light of basal area. Generally speaking, if the basal area increases the density would decrease, the number of trees would be fewer. But here in Beall Woods, in both the upland and the bottomland, there isn't as much of a decline of density as one would think from this tremendous basal area. In other words, it is an extremely dense woods in addition to having this high basal area, greater than the excellent Hoot Woods or Allee research forest.

Q. You have made these investigations yourself?

A. Yes. May I add some more? I think this is all the more note-worthy in view of the fact that Indiana is primarily a forested state whereas Illinois is a prairie state, yet here in this one stand in your state we found much superior quality to anything we have in our forested state.

*   *   *

This testimony held firm under protracted cross-questioning by opposing counsel. The trial continued into the afternoon, but at lunch that day, when the confident pro-park forces ate together, Dr. Olmsted told the group that as soon as he had heard my testimony he knew that our side was going to win. Indeed, the judge ruled in favor of the state, which soon afterward paid the very temporary owner the amount of the appraisal.

Beall Woods Nature Preserve was established, with trails through it for public use as I and the other conservationists had suggested in our testimony. A large, old barn near the woods was remodeled for a museum and information center, wholly in character with the environment. Later the National Park Service designated the preserve as a National Natural Landmark. Beall Woods belongs to us all, and to the future.

40

CHAINS OF CHANGE IN ECOSYSTEMS

"THE CREATION of the new science of ecosystem ecology is, without doubt, the most important single event that has happened in the twentieth century." This evaluation is given by Dr. S. Dillon Ripley, the Secretary of the Smithsonian Institution; he takes a much longer-term view than most of us.

Compared with other life sciences, ecology had a delayed birth and in adolescence suffered reluctant acceptance by other scientists and the public. American interest in it began in Nebraska, and picked up a few years later when in 1901 Chicago botanist Henry C. Cowles described the course of plant succession in the dunelands along the south shore of Lake Michigan. The chief site of his pioneer study is now a special nature preserve within an Indiana state park on the lakeshore. A young naturalist who lived at the edge of these dunes, James D. Watson, was to find in the special biota there the inspiration for a biological career that led to his discovery with Francis Crick of the double helix configuration of the hereditary material DNA.

Although Sir Arthur Tansley introduced the term "ecosystem" in 1935, he failed to follow up the implications of this concept. Aside from the evolutionary theory it shared with all biology, ecology entered the Forties without a validated conceptual framework with generally accepted generality and consequence. The chief reason for this was that ecologists more often studied *structure*, at higher levels of integration where ecology uniquely operates, than *function* at those same levels.

A young graduate student was to change all this during what became for him an agonizing race against mortality.

Raymond L. Lindeman was born on July 24, 1915, in Redwood County, Minnesota, and as a boy became interested in natural history. In 1936 he began graduate work and a teaching assistantship at the University of Minnesota, majoring in zoology and minoring in botany. He was almost the earliest of the many scientists who have done important work at Cedar Creek Bog Lake, a small lake in a late stage of succession and surrounded by much wild land. He first published some of his results when he was 24.

In failing health but with unflagging courage, he continued studying this shallow, senescent lake. His professors recognized his brilliance; although they did not understand what he was about, they let him follow a different drummer. During his long days on the water, always helped by his wife Eleanor, he collected specimens and data and mulled over what they meant. He came to understand that by combining the physical stage-setting with the community of life it supports, ecologists may learn the mode of operation of the highest integrated level in Nature, the ecosystem, and that this unit, not the cell, is the fundamental unit of study in ecology.

He traced food-chains very thoroughly through the lake ecosystem, determining the origin, course, and fate of both the material substances involved and their content of energy.

He untangled the basic principles of living organisms with relation to the second law of thermodynamics, particularly. The cycling and recycling of material substances, and the stepwise degradation of energy derived from sunlight and decreasing in amount as used at higher and higher nutritive levels to the top-most predator in the food chain, was all grist for his mental mill. He recognized different classes of organisms, functionally, as producers, (nearly invariably green and photosynthetic), consumers, decomposers, and transformers. He gave much attention to productivity at the different nutritive levels in the ecosystem. During long hospital stays he had much time to think.

Ray was blind in one eye, suffered from stomach ulcers so that he never drank anything stronger than milk, and finally was brought down by a rare and inadequately diagnosed form of hepatitis while he was doing post-doctorate work at Yale. The last and most important of his six technical papers was at first rejected by the major American ecological journal. Finally published by that journal in 1942, it justified the modern, simple definition of ecology as the science of the structure and function of Nature. An obituary of the author appeared as an addendum to his paper. Although he did not live to see his seminal paper in print, he did know that it was accepted. His body was left to the Yale Department of Anatomy. Without having reached his twenty-seventh birthday, Lindeman initiated the synthesis that clarifies the comment by mystic Frederick Elder, "Life on Earth has many facets, but the important point is that all facets are part of the same diamond."

Today the University of Minnesota supports a 5,500-acre research center that includes Cedar Creek Bog Lake. This preserved tract is honored as a National Natural Landmark by the National Park Service. In the main building of the modern laboratory complex, only a heroic stone's throw from the little lake, a portrait of Lindeman at age twenty-three is prominently displayed. Four of us hiked along the lakeshore, our spirits soaring with the mass flight of a yellow and black dragonfly species emerging first from the shallow water, then from their nymphal shells which remained clinging empty to the rushes. They reminded us of Ray Lindeman's frail shell, left behind when the living creations of his mind took wing into the bright sky of human thought.

Lindeman's successors are concerned with learning and applying the rules of a vital game—the rules that a dedicated

young man first began to unravel. For there is always in play a dramatic and desperate game of planetary tennis. The ball, made of substances and energy, is volleyed back and forth between the opposing teams. In this court are Life and Order, in that one Death and Disorder. The net and court markings, which delimit and control the alternation, represent the familiar laws of thermodynamics. These energy laws, knowledge of which distinguishes ecological scientists from traditional naturalists of past times, constitute the only general morality that Nature knows. Nature may seem wasteful and heedless of life, but she is an alert referee who keeps her eye on the ball more than on the players, and enforces the rules strictly and fairly. To enjoy the skill and beauty of the play is everyone's privilege. To learn its technical rules and to help insure that the knowledge is used beneficially to man and Nature are the ecologists's duties and pleasures.

EPILOGUE

THE APPROACHING SPLENDOR

EVEN though most people live more than a decade and very few live as long as a century, convenience has dictated our use of the decimal system in dealing with time. Realistically, however, the expectable span of a human life now closely matches the interval between visits of Halley's Comet—seventy-six years. I call this more human unit of time the "halley." Many halleys ago, people in Europe used to pray, "Lord, save us from the Devil, the Turk, and the Comet!" One halley ago, some feared that, as the Earth passed through the comet's tail, earth-fires would ignite comet gases and our planet be seared in devastation. Today, human fears are more of man-made than of cosmic horrors.

Two of my ancestors, constituting one lap of the relay race of the generations, arrived in America just 4.78 halleys ago. My ultimate expectation is to live here at least 1.04 halleys, so that I may see the comet again as it next swings toward us. That would, I think, complete a natural, siderially-marked life span, without benefit of frenzied medical heroics or undignified organ transplantation designed to prolong life to a full century.

"The past," wrote Carl Sandburg, "is a bucket of ashes." But he couldn't have meant it, for he was an authority on Lincoln-era history. Besides, ashes can be quite revealing to archaeologists, vulcanologists, and detectives. In a society oriented to its youth, who possess little personal past, we over-value the present and future, and give the past an undeserved bad press. Those who disclaim interest in past events have relatively little to claim their attention; after all, everything that ever happened is now in past time.

If "the present" is an idea whose time has come, if it is the one over-riding reality, why is there no objective, generally accepted definition of it? To a geologist, the present is approximately the last ten thousand years. To the news reporter it is a couple of days, and to most of us it is perhaps a month or a year. In the most precise science, physics, is not the present defined operationally as the nanosecond or picosecond? The past presses upon the present from the rear, the future encroaches into it from the opposite direction, and between these irresistible forces the present is squeezed into infinitesimal brevity.

Three decades ago, a Nature preservation society talked of dedicating land reserves "in perpetuity." However, their attorney pointed out that perpetuity is a long time. Today, no one realizes more profoundly than environmentalists that only the past is battened down—the present is fleeting and the future uncertain. While my overall personal aim for the future is just to continue my support of neg-entropy, there is a more specific plan for one day to come.

It will be a clear, velvety evening, I hope, that evening of my seventy-ninth birthday, one suitable for a family party of celestial proportions. During my party we shall strictly avoid "dwelling" on or in the past. However, for our purpose, the present will be defined as the one-halley period between 1910 and 1986.

A few of our ten thousand color slides, the best of those depicting the family's history and travels and friends, may be projected during late afternoon, while the younger children are outdoors running after sun-dogs. I hope Elizabeth will relate how in driving across Florida on March 5, 1976, we were very surprised to see a fabulous comet at 4 AM, for we were unaware that any Comet named "West" existed until we were told of it as we entered Everglades National Park. I may read aloud some things I have written. Lately I have

208

been writing to kill time. This seems fair enough, for Time will eventually kill me.

Dinner will not consist of ordinary comestibles, but of the most delicate and exotic comet staples from the Cosmos. As twilight approaches, a lawn chair facing south will be set out for each one who is with us. The songbirds will quiet down and find shelter in the pine trees we had planted, 0.4 halleys before, on our parcel of planet. There will be desultory, but good, talk. Some of my father's well remembered stories and jokes will be retold. Other favorite people, also at rest after running their courses well, will be lovingly recalled. No objective observers will be present to judge whether the conversation is trivial or profound.

As darkness follows dusk, the topmost branches of our trees shudder in anticipation of the rising wind from Space. We two unobtrusively hold hands. Silence has fallen—no one wishes to intrude between another and his comet. It is not through our words that a visitor from the sun's far province affects us. The comet is not alien unless we ourselves are alien in the universe where we live.

The roosting birds rustle among the whorls of pine boughs which are silently but firmly weaving into life's textures the comet-like evanescence we know as Time.

It is now full darkness except for the faded stars, an unusual number of falling meteors, and the comet I have been waiting to see once more.

ILLUSTRATIONS BY CHAPTER NUMBER

Cover of Paperback version: Purchased from ornithologist Alden Loring in Ithaca NY in 1929, these binoculars were the author's first. In 1933 they were stolen by a native on Easter Island (Chapter 28), used by the thief until 1935, and recovered then during the author's second visit there.

1. "Origin of the Totem Pole," an unretouched photo (turned sidewise) of a treeless shoreline of Great Bear Lake north of the Arctic Circle.

2. In springtime the water from a thawing snowbank drips from a shrub.

4. A group of rock columns elevated by frost action above the general surface of the diorite sill capping Et Then Island, Great Slave Lake. The central, highest prism is the one with the most nearly perfect pentagonal cross-section.

5. Thomas Alva Edison, literary-naturalist John Burroughs, and Henry Ford at Edison's winter home and laboratory in Fort Myers FL. Ford's estate was adjacent to Edison's.

6. The Joseph Inman portrait of John James Audubon. Used by courtesy of Audubon Wildlife Sanctuary at the old Penn (Mill Grove) estate, Audubon PA, in the 1762 house which was Audubon's first home in America.

7. A wild but bold Gray Jay alights on Elizabeth Lindsey's hat in the high country on Mount Rainier's west flank.

8. All the western yellow (ponderosa) pines at this soil-free, droughty level of the Grants Lava Flow NM are much stunted, distorted, and ancient, whereas the same species above the sandstone escarpment beyond are growing normally.

9. *Lycopodium* growing in ring form along the Blue Ridge Parkway.

10. The original park museum of Mount Rainier National Park, at Longmire WA, is still used as such. It is now

dedicated as a historical landmark. Photo taken in 1933, when wildflowers were displayed on the porch, and the park naturalist's office, park library, herbarium, study skin collection, and darkroom were on the second floor.

15. Only John Burroughs and two packers accompanied President Theodore Roosevelt on a two-week tenting and birding tour of Yellowstone Park in 1903. Courtesy of National Park Service.

16. A stand of virgin hardwoods is preserved by the U. S. Forest Service at Pioneer Mothers Memorial Forest (Cox Woods) near Paoli IN. Photo courtesy USFS.

18. Celebrated photographer of the American Indians, Edward S. Curtis took this picture in 1899 during the Harriman Alaska Expedition, at a Cape Fox village. From the rare Harriman Album, courtesy of Gov. W. Averell Harriman.

19. Edgemire, where a family of five modern pioneers homesteaded, building their cabin, outbuildings, and sauna at the lakeside where a kayak is tied at the dock.

20. Compass card.

21. When the Lewis overthrust fault block pushed inexorably eastward, these sedimentary strata were folded like taffy. Erosion of that block resulted in the Front (Lewis) Range of the Rockies, including Chief Mountain, the easternmost remnant.

22. This rock island in a ponded "Jacob's Well" supports a sunken garden of rare *Asplenium* ferns accessible only by rope through a two-foot hole in the lava crust above. At times, algal (*Chlorella*) bloom floated on the doughnut-shaped pond.

23. Discoverer Charles Carroll emerges well-chilled from the "bottomless" ice cave at the summit rift of Chimney Mountain.

25. This modern house was built of terrones by an Indian family at Isleta Pueblo near Albuquerque NM. The surrounding wall is also of grass-brick construction.

28.   On Easter Island in 1933, the author rests against a supine statue on the seaward slope of Image Mountain, examining a human skull taken by a shipmate from a lava cavern nearby. Paul A. Siple photo, BAE II.

30.   Dr. Paul A. Siple started his notable career in antarctic exploration as the Eagle Scout on Richard Byrd's first South Polar trip in 1928-30. By arrangement, reprinted by permission from TIME, The Weekly Newsmagazine, Copyright Time Inc. 1956.

31.   The oaken icebreaker *Bear* moored to the sea ice of the Bay of Whales near Little America in 1934. Built in Scotland in 1874 for the U.S. search for Greeley, she long served the Coast Guard in Alaska, and went down in an Atlantic storm in 1963.

32.   A pair of husky dogs pictured during a brief rest of their seven-dog team while unloading supplies at Little America in 1934. BAE II photo.

34.   This batrachian species, undescribed and uncollected insofar as the author is aware, lives in crevices in a black lava flow several rods from busy U.S. 66 (now I-40), New Mexico's Acoma Indian Reservation. In both color and texture it mimics the dark lava surface.

36.   After sunset in the foreground, Mount Rainier is bright with alpenglow. The central eminence, Columbia Crest, is the present summit (14,410 feet) but not the original one which was much higher. Courtesy of former Park Naturalist, Prof. C. Frank Brockman.

37.   Photo-comparison over 41 years in Indian Henry's Hunting Ground. Photo at left (1933) shows one of the Mirror Lakes, but the 1974 picture shows it has disappeared, through natural drainage. Boulders near the old water margin are obscured or covered by subalpine fir growth and new soil built up by tundra vegetation.

38.   Giant sycamore on the Wabash River terrace in 1880. The man at left is Robert Ridgway, later Curator of Birds at the U.S. National Museum.

40.   The birthplace of esosystem science, Cedar Creek Lake was intensively studied by 24-year-old graduate student Raymond Lindeman. This senescent bog-lake is now a National Natural Landmark within a 5,500-acre research preserve. 40 end. In the Douglas fir-hemlock-western red cedar forest at Mount Rainier's western base, this miniature peak of red-brown prisms is what remains of a decayed western hemlock stump. It represents an end no more than a beginning in the cycle of continuing life in its ecosystem.

BIBLIOGRAPHY

Chapter 1: Tape, Walter. 1982. Folds, pleats, and halos. Am. Scientist 70: 467-474.

3: Pokagon, Simon. 1972 (1899). Queen of the Woods. Hardscrabble Books. Berrien Springs MI. 220 pp.

4: AAL (= A. A. Lindsey). 1952. Vegetation of the ancient beaches above Great Bear and Great Slave Lakes. Ecology 33: 535-549.

6: Beston, Henry. 1928. The Outermost House. Selwyn & Bount. London. 224 pp.

AAL. 1946. The nesting of the New Mexican Duck. The Auk 63: 483-492.

7: Siple, P. A. and AAL. 1937. Ornithology of the Second Byrd Antarctic Expedition. The Auk 54: 147-159.

10, 33, 40: AAL. 1974. The land resource base. In W. H. Johnson and W. C. Steere (Eds.). The Environmental Challenge. Holt, Rinehart and Winston. New York. 192-216.

10: Thompson, B. H. 1981. George M. Wright 1904-1936. The George Wright Forum (George Wright Society), Summer 1981: 1-4.

12: AAL and J. E. Newman. 1956. Use of official weather data in spring time-temperature analysis of an Indiana (Deam's Arboretum) phenological record. Ecology 39: 812-823.

13: Muir, John. 1965 repr. The Story of My Boyhood and Youth. Univ. of Wisconsin Press. Madison. 228 pp.

Porter, G. S. 1912. Moths of the Limberlost. Doubleday Page. New York. 369 pp.

Porter, G. S. 1912. Laddie. Doubleday Page. 602 pp. (Her most autobiographical fiction; rural life at end of the pioneer period).

15: Cutright, P. R. 1956. Theodore Roosevelt, the Naturalist. Harper. 297 pp.

Burroughs, John. 1907. Camping and Tramping with Roosevelt. 110 pp.

AAL. 1977. Was Theodore Roosevelt the last to see wild Passenger Pigeons? Proc. Indiana Acad. Sci. 88: 349-356.

Roosevelt, Theodore. 1978 (1888). Illus. by F. Remington. Ranch Life and the Hunting Trail. Bonanza. New York. 186 pp.

16: Crankshaw, W. B., S. A. Qadir, and AAL. 1965. Edaphic controls of tree species in presettlement Indiana. Ecology 46: 688-698.

AAL, W. B. Crankshaw, and S. A. Qadir. 1965. Soil relations and distribution map of the vegetation of presettlement Indiana. Botan. Gazette 126: 155-163.

AAL and L. K. Escobar. 1976. Eastern Deciduous Forest Vol. 2 Beech-Maple Region. Natural History Theme Studies No. 3. National Park Service. 238 pp.

AAL. 1968. Role of the individual ecologist in natural area preservation. Bioscience 18: 421-424.

AAL, D. V. Schmelz, and S. A. Nichols. 1969. Natural Areas in Indiana and their Preservation. Repr. 1970 by Am. Midland Naturalist, Notre Dame Univ., Notre Dame, Indiana. 605 pp.

16, 17: AAL. 1966. The Indiana of 1816; 18 pp. *in* AAL (Ed.) Natural Features of Indiana. Indiana Sesquicentennial Volume. Indiana Acad. Sci. (Repr. by) Am. Midland Naturalist, Univ. of Notre Dame, Notre Dame IN. 629 pp.

17: AAL and J. O. Sawyer, Jr. 1971. Vegetation-climate relationships in the eastern United States. Proc. Indiana Acad. Sci. 80: 210-214.

18: Burroughs, John. 1904. Far and Near. Houghton Mifflin. Boston. (Mainly his official narrative of the Harriman Alaskan Expedition.) 288 pp.

Goetzmann, W.H. and K. Sloan. 1982. Looking Far North. Viking Press. New York. 244 pp.

20, 33, 40: AAL. 1974. Land misuse and the land ethic. *In* W. H. Johnson and W. C. Steere (Eds.) The Environmental Challenge. Holt, Rinehart and Winston. New York. pp. 217-237.

22: AAL. 1945. Unique habitat for maidenhair spleenwort. Am. Fern Journal 35: 109-113.

AAL. 1949. An optical effect in *Chlorella* bloom in nature. Ecology 30: 504-511.

AAL. 1951. Vegetation and habitats in a southwestern volcanic area. Ecological Monographs 21: 227-253.

25: AAL. 1948. Terron vegetation in New Mexico. Ecology 29: 470-478.

26: Sawyer, J. O. and AAL. 1971. Vegetation of the Life Zones in Costa Rica. Indiana Acad. Sci., State Library, Indianapolis. 223 pp.

27: Harding, Walter. 1982. The Days of Henry Thoreau: A Biography. Dover (repr.). New York. 498 pp.

28-32: Byrd, R. E. 1935. Discovery. G. P. Putnam's. New York. 405 pp.

30: AAL. 1937. The Weddell seal in the Bay of Whales, Antarctica. Journal Mammalogy 18: 127-144.

Siple, P. A. 1936. Scout to Explorer: Back with Byrd in the Antarctic. G. P. Putnam's. New York. 239 pp.

Siple, P. A. 1959. 90° South. G. P. Putnam's. New York 384 pp.

33: Carson, Rachel. 1962. Silent Spring. Houghton Mifflin. Boston. 368 pp.

Leopold, Aldo. 1949 (and later reprints). A Sand County Almanac. Oxford Univ. Press. New York. 226 pp.

AAL. 1965. Our environment—exploitation or renewal? Concern (General Board of Christian Social Concerns, Methodist Church). 7 (2): 8-11.

33, 39: AAL. 1970. Is there intelligent life on Earth? *In* Stewardship Yearbook for 1971. National Council of Churches, p. 30-35.

34: Krutch, J. W. 1952. The Desert Year. Viking Press. New York. 270 pp.

Krutch, J. W. 1972 repr. The Voice of the Desert. Wm. Sloane Associates. 223 pp.

38: AAL, R. O. Petty, D. K. Sterling, and W. VanAsdall. 1961. Vegetation and environment along the Wabash and Tippecanoe Rivers. Ecological Monographs 31: 105-156.

39: AAL. 1963. Analysis of an original forest of the lower Wabash flood plain and upland (Beall Woods, IL). Proc. Indiana Acad. Sci. 72: 282-287.

40: Lindeman, R. L. 1942. The trophic-dynamic aspect of ecology. Ecology 23: 399-419.

AAL. 1980. The ecological way. (Lindeman's story). Naturalist. Spring 1980: 1-9.

APPENDIX

MERRY LEA ENVIRONMENTAL LEARNING CENTER OF GOSHEN COLLEGE

In 1938 Lee A Rieth, recently graduated as a civil engineer from Purdue University, was employed by the state of Indiana to conduct geological surveys. As he studied the area between and around Bear Lake and High Lake in Noble County, he was deeply impressed by the geology, flora, and fauna he found there. Since 1963 Lee and Mary Jane Rieth have been purchasing parcels of land adjacent to the lakes, with the aim of assembling a large tract for nature preservation and public educational use. The result is the Merry Lea Environmental Learning Center which the Rieths founded in 1967. Today it comprises about 900 acres of forests, lakeshores, oldfields, ponds, streams, marshland, and limy prairie. Almost from the founding of Merry Lea the author of this book served as scientific advisor to the organization.

More recently through collaboration with The Nature Conservancy, the Indiana Department of Natural Resources Division of Nature Preserves, and Goshen College, preservation and suitable use of the area is permanently assured. Ownership is now held by Goshen College, an undergraduate liberal arts institution located in Goshen, Indiana, and affiliated with the Mennonite Church.

The college administers, maintains, and operates the center to provide year-round educational and recreational programs. Not only families and individuals, but also schools, colleges, civic, social, and religious groups utilize the natural features and the buildings. Membership in the Friends of Merry Lea is open to all interested in nature and the conservation of land and life, but it is not a requirement for occasional visits. Members receive a regular newsletter and discounts for center activities. Volunteer assistance of many different kinds is welcomed at Merry Lea; the writing and editing of this book and the financing of its printing and binding are examples of support by volunteers and donors. The Learning Center is located one mile north of the Intersection of county roads 350S and 500W just off state route 109 south of Wolf Lake, IN. Inquiries may be addressed to Larry R. Yoder, Director, Merry Lea Center, Goshen College, Goshen, IN 46526.

ACKNOWLEDGMENTS

My wife Elizabeth S. Lindsey, whose role in many of the episodes related was indispensible, assisted in proofreading the computer printouts which our daughter Louise L. Becker had cheerfully prepared from my typed manuscript, and read the page proofs. Mr. and Mrs. Lee A. Rieth very generously financed the printing and binding of this book. Dr. Robert Owen Petty read certain of the chapters and made many helpful suggestions.

Thanks are also extended to those who permitted use of their comments as promotional endorsements. The few chapter-head-piece photographs not taken by the author are credited in the list of photo legends above. I am grateful also to the following persons and institutions for aid or encouragement: Astronomical League, Mary Fuertes Boynton, C. Frank Brockman, George Wright Society (Robert M. Linn and Durward L. Allen), W. Averell Harriman, David P. Johnston, Enda Mills Kiley, Eric Klinghammer, Holley Lantz, Donald B. Lawrence, Library of Congress, David and Joan Lindsey, Margaret (Mardy) Murie, National Archives, National Museum of Natural History, National Park Service, New York Geological Society, Raphael L. Rodriguez, Nathan Skallman, and the U. S. Bureau of Land Management.

PERMISSIONS

My headpiece photopair for Chapter 37, and a paragraph or so of the text of my article, was reprinted by permission from *National Parks and Conservation Magazine*, November. Copyright © 1977 by National Parks and Conservation Association.

The quote from Governor Harriman and several sentences of mine are reprinted from the June 1978 issue of *Bioscience*, Vol. 28, No. 6, p. 383-386.

The W. E. Rogers photo of a *Rhododendron maximum* inflorescence is used as illustration for Chapter 12, being reprinted from the 1965 reissue, page 431, of Rogers' *Tree Flowers of Forest, Park, and Street* by permission of Dover Publications, Inc.

The permission statement for use of TIME Magazine cover painting of Dr. Siple appears under "30" in the Illustrations list.

Most of the material herein has not been published previously. However, certain bits and pieces from the author's articles in popular magazines, reworked into briefer and often less technical form, are used by permission of these periodicals to which I also extend thanks: *Natural History*, (American Museum of Natural History, © 1949, 1977), *Naturalist*, and *Science Digest*.

ABOUT THE AUTHOR

The author is a Purdue University ecologist, and writer of six previous books including the first one on the natural areas and nature preserves of any of our states (Indiana). After graduation from Allegheny College, he earned his Ph.D. in botany, ornithology, and entomology at Cornell University. He served as the vertebrate zoologist with the Byrd Antarctic Expedition of 1933-35, overwintering at Little America, and much later investigated tundra vegetation at the opposite end of the Earth for the Canadian and U. S. governments. He has also done ecological work in deserts, mountains, coasts, and the tropics, but his chief research interest is in the vegetation of the Midwest.

In 1976, Dr. Lindsey received the Eminent Ecologist Award. He is the first professional managing editor of *Ecology* and *Ecological Monographs*, edited the *Proceedings of the Indiana Academy of Science*, and for twenty years was plant ecology editor for *Biological Abstracts*. A new animal genus, and a group of fifteen islands off the coast of the Antarctic Continent were named for him. He holds a Special Congressional Medal, and a number of conservation and science education awards. His recent popular writings appear in *Natural History*, *Science Digest*, *National Parks*, and the *Journal of the Theodore Roosevelt Association*, and in a new Readers Digest volume on American wildlife. More detailed biographical information may be found in the Marquis reference book *Who's Who in the World*.